Major

Religions

of the

World

Major Religions of the World

Marcus Bach

ABINGDON PRESS

NEW YORK   NASHVILLE

MAJOR RELIGIONS OF THE WORLD

Copyright, 1959, by The Graded Press

c

To Mr. Shirley Mitchell

FOREWORD

The world has suddenly become a close neighborhood. Incredible speed of travel, new media of instantaneous communication, the reality of flight into outer space, have drawn the citizens of the good earth into an intimacy unique in history.

There are no longer any strange lands around the globe— no foreign frontiers—no uncharted areas or isolated people. What men think and how men live are common concerns. And in this new and wonderful world, man's quest for truth and his awareness of God have taken on a new dimension.

There is a growing conviction among thinking people everywhere that an era of peace and understanding is in the making. The basis of this new era must be spiritual. It will need to be built upon a renewed will to believe that faith can conquer fear and that love will triumph over hate. This belief moves like a subterranean stream beneath all the gloomy talk about the cold war and power politics, and it is steadily rising to reality in the hearts of men.

Because religiously-minded people of the world are drawing closer together, they are also demanding to know more about each other's faith. Not that their beliefs should or must be watered down, but they must be re-examined, explored anew, and *lived* as they have never been lived before.

All of this makes it a time of immense challenge for all religions, especially Christianity. We who have emulated the Christ in word are now being asked to demonstrate him in deed. We of the great profession are now being called upon to practice his principles in the light of our time. We can do this most effectively through personal dedication when we

7

understand Christianity's place among the major religions of the world.

Wherever I go along the far reaches of Church Street, U.S.A., people are asking pertinent questions: "In what way are we like the people of other faiths and in what ways are we different? What are our distinctives? What is the nature of religious knowledge and how does it affect the lives of men? What can I learn from others and what can they learn from me?" Let us, they say in all good faith, see whether some of the things we quarreled about were the result of communication difficulties, semantic problems, and the failure to honestly spell out and discuss what we truly believe.

In this compact and intimate world, religion or the lack of it is continually at the heart of man's thought. The story of mankind, as this popularly-written book will show, is the record of man's belief. Certainly in the realm of religion which is life's most vital field of study, it is essential to know exactly where we stand in our relationship to God, to others, and to ourselves.

So come along on this adventure. You will then realize that we understand people best when we understand what they believe. And as you join in this research you, too, will realize that the more we can do to make collective the dispersed spiritual potential of people everywhere, the deeper will be our faith and the more secure will be tomorrow's world for us and for all men everywhere.

MARCUS BACH
Destiny Bay
Boswell, B.C.
Canada
1959

CONTENTS

CHAPTER   PAGE

1. Ever the Quest   11

2. Hinduism—Religion of the One God
    Who Is Many   21

3. Zoroastrianism—Religion of Good and Evil   33

4. Buddhism—Religion of the Eightfold Path   47

5. Judaism—Religion of a Divine Destiny   61

6. Confucianism and Taoism—Religion of
    Good Ethics   74

7. Shinto—Religion of the Way of the Gods   85

8. Islam—Religion of the Book   97

9. Christianity—Religion of the Revelation
    of God in Christ   111

10. Your Religion and You   121

Index   127

1

Ever the Quest

THE history of religion is the thrilling story of man's upward climb to God. Man's search is so sincere, his need so great, and his discovery so important that nothing in the world is more vital than the spiritual quest.

Every culture and every people seek for divine truth, sing of their beliefs, and have their rites and rituals. No conviction is more universal, no theory more fundamental, than this: Life must have its origin in a divine Spirit or Source.

It is impossible to conceive of the universe without God, and one cannot visualize life without him as Creative Cause. Even a nation such as Russia, which officially says that God does not exist, is proclaiming him by its denial. The lowliest Russian peasant knows that he needs but look to the skies to discover that "the heavens declare the glory of God; and the firmament sheweth his handiwork" (Psalms 19:1, King James Version).

THE DESIRE TO WORSHIP

The impulse to worship lies deeply ingrained in the heart of every man. It defies opposition. It is bound to lead him in search for God.

11

To many people in other times and in other lands God has been symbolized in many ways. Some persons have thought of him as a mountain to be climbed, a height to be reached, or a summit to be conquered. We, too, are spiritual mountaineers. Sometimes when persons are asked why they must climb the mountain, their reply, like that of every other true adventurer, is, "Because it is there."

God is there. The Something higher and greater than ourselves is calling. Until we find him, we are living in the valley. Until we catch a glimpse of him, however fleeting, we are wandering in a void. Being joined to the Lord in one Spirit, said John Wesley, is the religion and the righteousness man thirsts after.

Out of early man's bold journey to find God—in his glorious adventure to reach the mountain peak of his experience—he joined with other men. Pilgrims they were—seekers of the upward way; and often, as they met upon the path, they built, as it were, base camps together. Here they exchanged ideas and confided their hopes, their questions, their fears, joys, and discoveries. Together they fashioned their altars and their shrines, and that, simply stated, is how organized religion began.

It began with persons who shared the common quest upon a common path. And because there were men with special spiritual talents and men with unusual insight and wisdom, ministers and teachers arose. Because there were men who seemed specially chosen of God, there were also prophets. In all religions, small or great, there were always the holy ones.

MANY SEEK FOR GOD

As far back as we can glimpse into time and space, there were many paths up the mountain and many camps along those paths. There were also many guides and showers-of-the-way. All were convinced that their path was best. All were searching, speculating, and finding the footprints of God. And always there was the summit—beckoning.

We Christians believe that a Special One came down from the summit to show us the way. He came as a man, but the Godlikeness of his nature could not be hidden. He came, and the glory of his presence illumined every path and fell upon every trail by which men climbed. We called him King of kings, Lord of lords, and Prince of Peace.

He spoke and walked with us. The path he revealed was straight and narrow and not always easy. But it was full of glory and high adventure. Never before or since did God come so near the hearts of men or reveal so much of himself as he did through the Christ. The lives he touched were changed. The situations he encountered were transformed. A new era began with his advent, and through him men saw that God was infinitely tender and boundless in love.

Though Christianity has yet to conquer the world, Christ conquered it. Though Christianity has yet to be fully lived, Christ lived it. Though Christianity has yet to finally prove the divine command, Christ proved it. Since he came, all other paths of faith have felt the impact of his presence; all people know that the God they seek is seeking them.

CHRIST, THE EVER-PRESENT LORD

Wherever man lives, man worships; and wherever man worships, there the Christ is standing, seeking to save. Because he loves all men, he stands beside the Hindu chanting his mantras and bowing his head at his shrine.

He lingers beside the Jew reading the Torah or contemplating the mezuzah on the doorpost of his home.

He pauses beside the Parsi bowing to the sacred fire in his secret temple.

He watches the follower of Confucius who reverently beholds the tablets of the temple, the Taoist burning incense on his golden altars, the Buddhist spinning the prayer wheels, and the Shintoist making his pilgrimages to the holy shrine.

He keeps his vigil over the Moslem kneeling on his prayer rug in the mosque, and he hears the echo of the imam as he calls, "There is no God but Allah."

He is interested in all sincere seekers after truth, even though they have not yet arrived at a full understanding of God.

Religion Expresses Many Things

Religion means different things to different men. To the primitive it means offering his animal sacrifices, and to the aborigine it means mutilating his body. It may be expressed in baptismal ceremonies for the dead and in spiritual exercises for the living. It is man attempting to prove the mystery of life and probing the riddle that death is but the lighted passage to another world.

Religion is the priest at his altar and the minister in his pulpit. It is the neophyte first learning the concepts of his faith and the penitent in his confession. It is a cross, a book, a candle, a hope, a song. It is work and play and even ceremonies for war and peace.

Religion is many things. But for the Christian it is finding God through Christ. Remembering this, our association with other men who walk other paths can help us find deeper meaning in our own faith.

We can look upon the religions of the world as a circle—a circle that, like truth, has no beginning and no end. We can visualize all denominational expressions and types of minds as arcs in the circle of truth. We can say that no one can claim the whole circle and that each can rightly claim some part of it. But for Christians the hub in the circle of truth is the knowledge that God is known most perfectly and understood most clearly through Jesus Christ.

Historian Arnold Toynbee expressed this conviction when he said in an interview, "I was brought up in the belief that my . . . religion held the key to the mystery of existence; but I have come back to the belief that this key is not held by my ancestral religion exclusively. Since this is the religion in which I have been brought up, my own and earliest approach to the mystery will always lie along this path. But this need not prevent me from also realizing that there are other paths which are for people bred in other traditions."

That is how it seemed to me. After tramping many religious trails for many years and following the paths of faith wherever they might lead, after trying to put myself in the place of people around the world who live and worship differently than I, I felt that the great religions should be viewed as different dialects by which man speaks to God—and God to man. The apostle Paul approaches this view in Romans 1:18-32, where he recognizes the universal revelation of God and judges other religions because they do not live up to the full revelation they possess. For him, of course, Christ was the final truth. To me, also, Christianity speaks most clearly; to others, their parental faith seems most meaningful and therefore constitutes for them the only path upward to the summit of God.

Among followers of every faith I found the mystical quality that hints of the Divine Presence. I learned that people in other religions also have a kind of communion and partnership with Something greater than ourselves. A sense of the

timeless undergirds their lives. Many are sensitive of others
and sometimes masters of themselves. They also have a secret
confidence, and this is worship. There are those who have
the joy of deepened security, which is the result of worship.
Some are living wholesome, spirited lives, which are the reward of worship. But always, as a Christian, I return to the
path our Master walked, and there I try to walk with him.

Therefore, when people ask me, "What has worshiping
with others done to your faith?" my answer is, "It has intensi-
fied it. The fellowship of other religions, wherever found, has
challenged my religion anew."

For I never think of worship without remembering that
at this very moment, somewhere in the world, a Jew is saying his prayers. Somewhere a Moslem is kneeling in his
mosque, a Parsi is tending his sacred fire, a Buddhist is bowing at his shrine, and a Hindu is chanting a mantra. Somewhere in a city, cathedral lights are burning. Somewhere in
a jungle, a mystical ritual is being performed. Each is seeking a pathway winding upward upon the mountain of God.
Religion is truly the eternal quest, manifested in various
forms.

RELIGION FACES NEW DEMANDS

Today, as if by a divine conspiracy, something new has
been added to our human relations. We are realizing that we
must learn to live together if anyone is going to live at all.
The forces of destruction, which have become capable of
total devastation, must now at last be matched by the forces
of spiritual might. Our vaunted phrase, "Only religion can
save the world," is finally being put to the test. The power
to kill which man has devised is causing him to re-examine
the power of love which God has wrought.

When Albert Einstein realized what had been done with his basic equations on the conversion of mass into energy, he stood aghast. Aware that man now held the destruction of the world in his hands, the great physicist went on the air shortly before his death to plead with the United States and Russia to do away with fear and mistrust. He emphasized the fact that the arms race invites men to destroy one another. Nothing can save man, he told the world in effect, except spiritual understanding.

Gaining spiritual understanding is the challenge for our time. The question is, How can we maintain denominational loyalties and at the same time develop a respect for the followers of other faiths? Theological exclusiveness has long been a feature of religious convictions. Many a path up the mountain has borne the warning: "Private road—for members only."

Today we realize that the deeper we sink our roots into the faith we love, the greater will be our appreciation of the quest of *all* people. An investigation of the other person's point of view should inspire in us a renewed desire for investigating our own ideas. It should also make us more concerned about supporting more effectively our own points of view.

Learning About Other Faiths

Let us, therefore, stand for a moment where others stand. Let us look at some other forms of spiritual experience through the eyes of those whose background has identified them with a culture and creed different from our own. Let us walk for a little while with those who make their way up the mountain along paths different from ours and see how like or unlike our own their paths may be. Albert Schweitzer reminds us that we should impart as much of our faith as we can to those who walk the road of life with us and accept as something precious that which comes back to us from them.

This expresses rather perfectly the purpose of this book. Let us be true to our tradition and our faith and let our light shine before men. But let us also be citizens of the whole spiritual world, concerned with life both in America and in Asia. Let us be prepared to accept whatever is good and beautiful and true wherever found, for there are those who will be finding the good and beautiful and true in us. The heart that searches is the heart that loves. And today the whole course of history is moving toward a united quest for the living reality of God.

· Our search in this study is to discover what each faith does in and for the lives of its adherents. We wish to see the role it plays in the fundamental problems every person must face, the basic questions every person asks, and the basic hopes toward which every person aspires. The various forms in which truth has been revealed, believed, and practiced have ever been the aspects of the universal search. Let us, for the moment, make these the sympathetic objectives of our quest.

Glossary

CHAPTER 2: HINDU TERMS *

Agni (ŭg'nĭ) The Vedic god of the altar fire and mediator between the gods and men.

atman (ăt'măn) The life principle, soul, or self.

Bhagavad-Gita (bŭg'à·vàd·gē'tä) A philosophical dialogue between Arjuna and Krishna which was probably written around the second or third century A.D. or earlier.

Brahma (brä'mà) The supreme soul or essence of the universe, immaterial, uncreated, illimitable, timeless. Brahma is conceived as comprising the trinity—Brahma, Vishnu, and Siva.

dharma (där'mà) Hindu religious law or doctrine; also religion or religious duty.

Ganesa (gà·nä'sà) The Hindu god of wisdom and prudence. He is represented as being a short red or yellow man with an elephant's head.

Hanuman (hŭn'ōō·män') The Hindu monkey god.

Hinduism (hĭn'dōō·ĭz'm) A religious and social system native to India.

Indra (ĭn'drà) The great national god of the Indo-Aryans. Persons who worship him believe that he is responsible for thunder and rain and that he overcomes his enemies and rewards his worshipers with booty gained as a result of victories.

karma (kär'mà) In Hinduism this term refers to the entire ethical consequences of a person's acts. These results are considered as fixing one's lot in his future existence.

Krishna (krĭsh'nà) The eighth incarnation of Vishnu and one of the most widely worshiped of the Hindu deities.

* Many of the words used in this book are peculiar to the particular faiths or religions discussed. For this reason they may not be familiar to the average reader. Because these words are basic to an adequate understanding of these faiths, brief definitions have been provided at the outset of each discussion.

19

Lakshmi (lŭk'shmē) The Hindu goddess of beauty and wealth. She is the consort of Vishnu.

maya (mä'yä) Magic; the power by which the physical world is created or made known.

Parvati (pär'wà·tē) A Hindu goddess who is considered as being the daughter of the Himalayas.

rishi (rĭsh'ĭ) An inspired Hindu poet or holy sage.

Sarasvati (sŭr'ás·wà·tē) The consort of Brahma and the goddess of learning, music, and speech.

Soma (sō'mà) The personification of the liquor of the soma plant, an East Indian leafless vine that yields a milky juice. In Hinduism this personification is worshiped as a god.

Upanishads (ōō·pän'ĭ·shădz) Speculative treatises dealing with the nature of man and the universe. These writings form a late part of Vedic literature. The earliest Upanishad probably dates from the eighth century before Christ.

Varuna (văr'ōō·nà) In Hinduism the supreme cosmic deity. He is considered as creator, ruler, and special guardian of the cosmic order.

Veda (vä'dà) The most ancient sacred literature of the Hindus. The term may refer specifically to one or all of four canonical collections of hymns, prayers, and liturgical forms which serve as the basis for all Vedic literature and religion.

Vishnu (vĭsh'nōō) The second god of the Hindu trinity, called "the Preserver."

yogi (yō'gē) A person who practices yoga; that is, the mental discipline of directing his attention exclusively upon one certain object—abstract or concrete—with the idea of establishing identification of consciousness with that object.

2

Hinduism
Religion of the One God Who Is Many

ONE day I saw a Hindu holy man sitting on the banks of
the Ganges in front of the statue of Krishna. How long
had he been gazing at this silent, wooden figure? Hours,
days, or perhaps weeks. He was in a trancelike state. His
body looked as if it were molded out of clay, and he himself
looked like an image. It seemed to me he had stopped breath-
ing.

My first impulse was to turn to my Hindu companion, a
well-dressed, scholarly young man, and ask, "Why does he
do this? How do you explain such idolatry?"

As if reading my thoughts, my companion said, "Who
knows by looking at the outward appearance of a man what
is in his heart?"

I never forgot these words as I traveled the subcontinent,
India. I recalled them whenever I saw the poor villagers buy-
ing a flower or a bit of fruit or bread outside the temple walls
and reverently placing their offering beside a statue or inside a shrine. I remembered the words when the Ramakrishna
monks ministered to the sick and served the needy, when the
disciples in the many ashrams chanted their prayers, when
the yogis performed their fantastic spiritual exercises, when

21

the temple worshipers chanted their prayers, and when India's most famous philosopher, Ramakrishna Paramahansa, spoke to me through his sayings about the religion of his people.

India—A Land of Philosophers

Wherever I went in India, I sensed the stirring heartbeat of a people's faith. From the breathless grandeur of the Taj Mahal to the unkempt hovel of the lowliest beggar, religion is a part of life. Scratch a Hindu and you find a philosopher. Listen and you will hear talk about the ways and wonders of the gods. Look and you will find a shrine in every village and the telltale signs of worship in nearly every home. This is Hinduism, the faith of 320,000,000 people who not only believe that they will live again but are convinced that they have lived before.

This doctrine of the wheel of life is one of the principal distinguishing characteristics of Hinduism. Whereas Christians believe that man's life is a three-act play—birth, death, and immortality—Hindus think in terms of an endless drama: birth, death, and rebirth; death and rebirth; death and rebirth. They insist that the soul has always existed and will continue to exist until it is merged with God, who is the Soul of Souls.

Basic Ideas

It can all be simplified, Hindus believe, if three basic truths are kept in mind.

The first is the law of identification, which can be stated in the old and oft-repeated Sanskrit phrase, *Tat twam asi,* which is to say, "That art thou," or "God and I are one," or "He who is yonder, yonder person, I am he."

In Hinduism the soul is everlasting in a sense that can hardly be grasped by the Christian mind. The fact that it survives the body is no mystery and no miracle, for it existed before the body was formed. "Never have I not been," says the god Krishna to a student. "Never hast thou not been, and never shall the time come when we shall not be."

The soul, according to Hinduism, is the *atman* or the only true self. All else is illusion or *maya*. The soul alone is real. A Western Christian mystic, Meister Eckhart, who was profoundly impressed by Hinduism, explained the law of identification by saying that the eye with which we see God is the same eye with which he sees us.

Every religious practice of the true Hindu is directed toward the realization of his oneness with God. To know oneself is to know God. To live as though the real "I" is eternal and indestructible is to live God. To discover that everything outside this reality is *maya* is to discover God. To grasp the full meaning of this oneness is to realize the essence of Hinduism.

This assumption on the part of a Hindu goes far beyond the customary Christian belief that our lives are a reflection of God's life, or that we are sons and daughters of God, or that God lives in us. To the Hindu the true self in each of us is the *atman*. It is *Tat twam asi,* and as the believing Hindu speaks the words out into the eternal void, he claims that an answer comes to him which says, "This and only this is truth."

KARMA

But there is a second truth called karma. We in the West usually translate *karma* loosely as meaning destiny or fate. We say that karma has something to do with "good breaks" or "bad breaks" or with things that just seem to happen. To the Hindu, however, karma is a law—an immutable law. A man is what he is, in respect to his fortune and his place in life, because of his karma.

Karma fixes the consequences of one's acts. It cannot be tampered with, altered, or destroyed. Karma, strictly speaking, is neither good nor bad. It simply *is*. We make it. Our past deeds and acts make it. We are *it*. Hindus believe that karma is the heart of the principle that we find in our Bible which says, "Do not be deceived; God is not mocked, for whatever a man sows, that he will also reap" (Galatians 6:7). Five thousand years before these words were written, the Hindu holy books had already said that a man becomes good by good deeds and bad by bad deeds.

A Hindu friend of mine, who loves the Christian faith and who is always trying to find parallelisms between his religion and mine, said to me, "Karma is just another way of saying, 'But seek first his kingdom and his righteousness, and all these things shall be yours as well.' We believe these words implicitly. Karma is a matter of spiritual law, regardless of what name we give it."

Once when I was riding in a taxi with a Hindu, we saw a man dying at the side of the road. We stopped to see what could be done, but the man was beyond help. "It is karma," said my friend. And I thought to myself, That is how Hindus explain everything in the world—suffering, blessings, sorrow, joy, low caste, high caste, pauper and priest, poor man, rich man. Karma covers all of life and assures the individual that what he is at any given moment is the consequence of what he has done at some previous moment. It is the operation of the law of cause and effect. It assures and warns man that nothing he does is ever lost, nothing is unaccounted for, nothing is forgotten, discarded, or irrelevant. Karma is an

eternally moving wheel that, like the mills of the gods, grinds
out men's destinies—and grinds "exceeding small."

REINCARNATION

Karma, however, in the Hindu mind, can never apply exclusively to this present life and the life to come, as Christians
might believe. Karma, in Hinduism, has an inseparable doc-
trinal companion called reincarnation.

Reincarnation is the third great truth for the Hindu.
It means "recurring life." It means that the soul of man—
the *atman* or life essence—is ever on a round of births and
rebirths. If a man dies, shall he live again? The Hindu
answers, "Yes, definitely. He will live again on this earth
to work out his destiny and to reap the reward of his previous acts."

Reincarnation answers many questions for the Hindu.
It explains the variety of personalities we find in the world,
the striking gap between the rich and the poor, between the
good and the bad, between the wise and the not-so-wise. It
explains all these seeming inequalities. It provides a solution
to the perplexing puzzle of why one person dies young;
another, old. It explains the phenomenon of a genius.

Even more than all these, the doctrine of reincarnation
prepares the Hindu for eventual union with God in a state
of immortal bliss. For this union is the aim and purpose of
life, and in birth after birth the soul of man has a chance
to eventually merge into the soul of God.

BELIEFS ABOUT GOD

What does a Hindu believe about God, and how do his
beliefs compare with those held by Christians?

Anyone who travels in India will be struck by the multi-
plicity of Hindu gods. There are literally thousands of gods.
There are gods within gods, families of gods, and wives and
children of gods. Here is Krishna, an embodiment or incarnation of Vishnu. Here, too, is Indra, god of the firmament;
Varuna, the all-seeing god; Agni, god of fire; Soma, personification of the juice of the soma plant. Hinduism honors
Ganesa, the elephant god, and Hanuman, the monkey god. It
loves and respects Sarasvati, goddess of learning, and
Lakshmi, goddess of wealth, and Parvati, who is the wife
of the god Siva. Hinduism has gods and goddesses galore.

*But when we look at Hinduism from the Hindu's point
of view, all gods are but representations of the one true God.*
Hinduism insists that God is one though he is many. He is
one in the same way that humanity is one.

Who is the one God? Hinduism says he is Brahma. And if
you ask a Hindu to describe Brahma, you will be told,
"Brahma is the World Soul. He is Cosmic Consciousness.
He is the Immortal Atman or Breath of Life, the Absolute,
the Principle of Love and Law."

We Christians find it difficult to describe our God, too.
We also give God many names and identifications. We call
him Jehovah, Lord, Father almighty, God of gods, King
of kings. What would you say if someone said to you, "Describe God for me"?

You might say, "God is Jesus Christ," or "Jesus Christ
is God," or "God is Spirit."

You might say, "God is Love," or "He is my Father," or
"He is Justice, Mercy, Power, Compassion."

The Hindu would say to you that all these designations
are but a few of the many attributes of God.

We Protestant Christians do not believe in images, but
if we did, it is conceivable that we might personify these

attributes of God and make, let us say, an image or statue of Love, another of Justice, another of Power. That, Hindus claim, is what they have done. They have created representations of the attributes of Brahma and have personified them and given them names. But Brahma remains the supreme One—the timeless, limitless essence of the universe. Of course, there are many Hindus who worship the attributes, just as there are many Christians who worship the qualities of morality, love, wisdom, and power more than they do God.

The Hindu finds his representation of God on the level of his understanding. His concept of God or gods is dictated by his power of spiritual perception. Religion to him is always an experiment in living. It is something highly practical, not theoretical. It is more subjective than objective. You can believe in one god or in ten thousand gods and be a Hindu. You can be an agnostic and be a Hindu; and, in a pinch, you can be an atheist and be a Hindu, for Hinduism is as much a culture and a philosophy as it is a religion. But you cannot be a Hindu without continually speculating on the eternal questions: Who am I? Why am I here? Where am I going? And you cannot be a true Hindu without reminding yourself: *"Tat twam asi"*—"Yonder Person, I am He."

Ask a Hindu where and when his religion, which he calls *dharma,* began, and he will say, "It has always been."

HOLY WRITINGS

There is hardly any doubt about Hinduism's being the oldest religion in the world, and its underlying unity is found in its holy books. Its books rather than any human founders are the inspiration for its faith. And if you ask a Hindu, "Who wrote these books?" or "Who were the in-

spired instruments who recorded these spiritual truths?" he
will say simply, "They were written by the rishis—the holy
men appointed by the one God who is many."

One day in Bombay a bearded, bespectacled Hindu came
to me at my hotel. From beneath his white shawl, which he
wore flung over his white Indian garb, he drew out a large,
beautifully bound book.

"Accept this as a gift," he said, "and as a remembrance
of your visit to our country. It will have special value for
you because it is one of the very first illustrated copies of our
beloved Bhagavad-Gita."

The man was Parmanand Mehra, artist and printer, who
had just published this significant edition of the holy book
that millions love. For the Hindu it is a kind of family Bible
and is rich in allegory, parable, and mystical thought. It is
part of the famous Mahabharata—the Great Story—which,
with the Ramayana, constitute Hinduism's immortal epics.

The theme of the Bhagavad-Gita is stated almost at the
very beginning when Arjuna, the disciple, asks the god
Krishna to tell him how he can recognize a man who knows
truth; that is, how he can identify an illumined person.

Krishna replies, in effect, "A man who is not affected by
achievement or failure, who is free from emotions such as
fear, anger, pride, vanity, jealousy, hate; a man who has disciplined his mind—he is wise; he is illumined." There is little
wonder that the artist Parmanand said with affection, "East
and West will understand each other better through the
pages of this book."

THE VEDAS

To the Bhagavad-Gita must be added the holy Vedas, the
most ancient and sacred of Hindu scriptures. There are four

canonical collections in this field: The Rig-Veda, containing over a thousand hymns; the Yajur-Veda, rich in hymns and prayers; the Sama-Veda, a book of revelation and chants and services; the Atharva-Veda replete with incantations.

"Veda" means spiritual wisdom, and the Vedas are so rich in knowledge and advice that historians refer to the time in which they were formulated as the "Vedic period"—about 1500-800 B.C. Their beauty reminds us of the glory of the Old Testament. The Rig-Veda is five times as long as the Psalms, and any one of its songs reveals its majesty:

> He knows the path of birds that fly through heaven, and,
>   sovereign of the sea,
> He knows the ships that are thereon.
> . . . .
> He knows the pathway of the wind,
> The spreading, high, and mighty wind;
> He knows the gods who dwell above.
>
> Varuna, true to holy law, sits down among his people; he,
> Most wise, sits there to govern all.
>
> From thence perceiving, he beholds all wondrous things,
>   both what hath been
> And what hereafter will be done.

The Upanishads

The "New Testament" of Hinduism is the Upanishads. These mystical writings consist of 108 poems dealing with the search for meaning in life and the universe. They are highly inspirational, philosophical, and, coming as they do at the end of the Vedas, are often referred to as Vedanta, or the end of Vedic Wisdom.

An example of the glory of the Upanishads may be found in the words:

He who sees himself in all beings,
And all beings in himself,
He enters the supreme Brahma
By this means and no other.

It is in the Upanishads that the principle of reincarnation and the doctrine of karma are philosophically explained. It is here that Hindus are reminded that the true self is the atman and that God is Atman and that the inner self and the Absolute Self are one. To unite the individual with Brahma and to join all Hindus into one mystical family of believers is the nature and purpose of the Upanishads.

HINDUISM EXPRESSED IN MANY WAYS

Hinduism is many things. It is the influence of the late Mohandas K. Gandhi, who, renouncing worldly goods and proclaiming that his people could not truly serve God while politically enslaved, instigated a movement that eventually made India free. It is also the faith of a Vinoba Bhave, disciple of Gandhi, who for many years has been trudging from village to village, persuading rich landowners to divide their farms among the poor. Bhave said to me, "What the world desperately needs is changed lives—lives that will demonstrate stewardship and honor God through sharing."

Hinduism is the work of various monastic orders made up of men who have started orphanages and schools, hospitals, and rehabilitation centers throughout India and in many parts of the world. These men have been inspired by Ramakrishna and Swami Vivekananda, Hindu saints. It is the selfless effort of a Dr. M. Modi, India's famous eye specialist, who once said, "The people are my God. The operating room is my temple, and the surgical instruments are my *pujah*."

Hinduism is the teaching and interpretation of India's

greatest theologian, Shankaracharya, the philosophy of India's Sarvepalli Radhakrishnan, the faith of Jawaharlal Nehru, the poetry of Rabindranath Tagore, the spiritual mysticism of a Sri Aurobindo, the service of a Swami Sivananda, the love and gentleness of the Hindu holy man T. L. Vaswani.

Hinduism is the practice of the yogi and the trancelike state of the holy men who sit on the banks of the sacred Ganges. It is the work of scholars in India's many universities and the faith of India's teeming millions who walk the city streets and villages and roam the hills and forests of this fabulous land. Hinduism is all this; and, most of all, it is the hope of those who, even as you and I, feel within their hearts the call of God.

A touch of Hinduism came into our home recently when a young swami from the Himalayas spent two weeks with us. He was typically Hindu: quiet, reflective, mellow, passive. He ate no meat, eggs, fish, garlic, or onions. His day began at 4 A.M. with an hour of yoga exercises and prayer. He came to America to "slow us down." I think we may have speeded him up! But the conviction that all life is God's life, and that God is as real as the air he breathes and the ground on which he walks, had a good effect on all who met him.

When, as he was leaving, he stood before us in his saffron robe to say "good-by," he touched the palms of his hands together and prayed:

"Thou [God] art the cherished guest in every household— father, brother, son, friend, benefactor, guardian, all in one. Deliver, mighty Lord, thy worshipers; purge us from the taint of sin; and when we die, deal mercifully with us on that final day!"

So say the Vedas. And so says Hinduism when it prays to the God in whom it believes and to the many gods who help explain the One.

Glossary

CHAPTER 3: ZOROASTRIAN TERMS *

Ahura-Mazda (ä'hŏŏ·rȧ·mäz'dȧ) In Zoroastrianism the supreme deity, the principle of good, the creator of the world, and guardian of men.

Amesha-Spenta (ä'mĕ·shȧ·spĕn'tȧ) One of seven archangels of Zoroastrianism.

Aryan (âr'ĭ·ăn) An Indo-European.

Avesta (ȧ·vĕs'tȧ) The sacred books of ancient Zoroastrianism.

Holy Heptad (hō'lĭ hĕp'tăd) Holy Seven; the Amesha-Spentas.

Magi (mā'jī) A priestly caste of ancient Persia.

Parsi (pär'sē) One who believes in Zoroastrianism, the ancient religion of Persia.

Zoroaster (zō'rō·ăs'tẽr) or **Zarathustra** (ză'rȧ·thōōs'trȧ) Founder of Zoroastrianism.

Zoroastrianism (zō'rō·ăs'trĭ·ăn·ĭz'm) The religion of Persia previous to the time when most of the people were converted to Islam. It is a dualistic religion; that is, it teaches that Ahura-Mazda, the lord of light and goodness, carries on a ceaseless war against Ahriman and the hosts of evil.

---

* Many of the words used in this book are peculiar to the particular faiths or religions discussed. For this reason they may not be familiar to the average reader. Because these words are basic to an adequate understanding of these faiths, brief definitions have been provided at the outset of each discussion.

3

Zoroastrianism
Religion of Good and Evil

ONE of my secret ambitions had always been to get inside a Zoroastrian temple. Ever since my first study of religions, I had been fascinated by accounts surrounding these mysterious places of worship.

It was reported that within the forbidden walls—forbidden to non-Zoroastrians—a sacred fire burned perpetually. I had been told that a special room was reserved for weird ceremonies for the dead and that the corpse was eventually carried to a tower where vultures devoured the flesh. I had heard that a white bull was kept within the temple court and that the Zoroastrians worshiped him. Evidently no outsider had ever gotten inside to discover whether or not these things were true.

ZOROASTRIANISM, JUDAISM, AND CHRISTIANITY

Other features about the faith were equally fascinating. It was said to be the oldest living religion in the world. And this must be true if we are thinking in terms of religions with definite founders. The mystery as to just when the founder lived has never been solved. Some scholars in the field of

religion set the birth of Spitama Zoroaster at six thousand
years before the birth of Jesus Christ. Others say he was
born six hundred years before the Christian Era. All insist
that Judaism and Christianity owe a great debt to this Persian
seer, Zoroaster, because he proclaimed many truths that Jewish prophets and Jesus himself reiterated.

For example, in the Avesta, as the sacred scriptures of
the Zoroastrians are called, it is stated that the world was
created in six days and that a man named Mashya and a
woman named Mashyoi were placed in a garden called Paradise and then driven out because they disobeyed God.

These ancient writings, originally recorded on twelve
thousand calfskins and bound with rings of gold, also taught
that there is an abode called heaven and a place called hell
and that God is a spirit whom men should worship "in spirit
and in truth."

Similarity between certain sayings of Zoroaster and the
words of Jesus were even more startling. Long centuries before the Galilean began his ministry, Zoroaster was already
proclaiming a golden rule that said that a man is good only
when he is willing not to do to another whatever is not good
for himself.

Before Jesus' teachings concerning the goodness of the
Father, Zoroaster described God as "the Giver of all good
and perfect things."

Hundreds of years before Golgotha, Zoroaster spoke about
the "resurrection from the dead," the "immortality of the
soul," and even went so far as to say that people who believed
in him (Zoroaster) "would not perish, but be given everlasting life."

The Wise Men from the East who followed the star and
brought their gifts to Bethlehem were Magi from Persia—
Zoroastrians who had been divinely informed that a Savior

had been born. All this was surely sufficient to recommend the faith for further study.

THE ZOROASTRIAN FAITH TODAY

I went to Bombay where the majority of the world's 140,000 Zoroastrians live because I wished to learn directly from them something about the mystery and meaning of their religion. Here in India the followers of Zoroaster are called Parsis, which means Persians. This was the simple term applied to their ancestors who, in the eighth century, fled their homeland in the face of fierce persecution by the Moslems who ruled Persia at the time.

The first thing that impressed me was the fact that, despite talk about fire worship and bulls in the temple and strange and sinister rites, the Parsis are among the best educated, most industrious, most cultured and charitable people of the subcontinent. I realized again how true it is that what we learn from the followers of a faith is considerably different from what we learn from books.

AN INSPIRED PROPHET

As far as the Parsis are concerned, they look upon Zoroaster (or Zarathustra, as he is known by his Avestan name) as a truly inspired prophet. Born in or near Azerbaijan, he was the son of a camel merchant named Porushaspa Spitama and his wife Dukhdav. He grew up in Persia at a time when the people worshiped many gods—Aryan nature gods and other gods to whom altars were built and sacrifices were made.

The boy Zoroaster, like many a boy after him for thousands of years to come, pondered and dreamed about religion. He

seldom saw the image of a god or breathed the hypnotic
incense without trying to figure out which god was greatest,
which priest was right, or which holy word should be believed.

He had the advantage of an excellent education, having
studied with some of the most learned teachers in Persia. It
is said he was a student from his seventh year until his
seventeenth.

At twenty Zoroaster withdrew from the world to pursue
the riddle of religion and to follow the quest wherever the
quest might lead. In the market places he listened to men,
and in the wilderness he listened to God. There were wars
in Persia caused by the invading Turanians, and many were
wounded. There was also much famine. Skilled in a knowledge of healing, Zoroaster gave his services freely to the
suffering people. Often he retired to a mountain—Mount
Sabalan—to pray.

At the age of thirty he was convinced that truth had been
revealed to him. He said that God had made himself known
in visions and that what he had seen, heard, and felt were,
for him, his most precious experiences.

Many Parsis are rich. They are well-to-do industrialists,
bankers, and businessmen of India. But they will tell you
that religion is their greatest treasure. Their temples, which
I wished to get into, and their teachings, which in so many
ways paralleled the teachings of Christ—these were their
ultimate riches, they said.

They invited me to witness a "thread ceremony," similar
in meaning to confirmation among Christians or *bar mizvah*
among Jews. In this case, the confirmand was a black-haired,
black-eyed boy of eight. In an impressive ceremony in his
father's garden on Malabar Hill in Bombay, he received from
the hands of the white-vested priest the sacred thread or

girdle tied around his waist. This signified that he was now prepared to take upon himself the duties, beliefs, and blessings of Parsiism. This is traditional among Parsi children—boys and girls alike—and has been the custom and ritual ever since Zoroaster began to preach his new faith.

What the Parsi priest told the boy on Malabar Hill in the presence of parents, relatives, and friends was what Zoroaster proclaimed in the midst of paganism and strife 2,500 years ago. Zoroaster claimed he had caught a glimpse of heaven. He had stood before the throne of one he called the "King of Kings." Like Moses he saw only a part of God, but he was given a name for God—the name all Parsis honor and revere: Ahura-Mazda, which means "God the Eternal Light."

THE SACRED SEVEN

Most Christians believe in three Persons in the Godhead: Father, Son, and Holy Spirit. They constitute the Trinity. Zoroastrians, however, believe there are *seven* persons in the Godhead. They constitute the Amesha-Spentas and are also referred to as the Sacred Seven, the Holy Heptad, or the Holy Immortals.

We Christians believe that the Trinity has its metaphysical counterpart in the life of man. Many consider God symbolical, of divine Power in the life of man. Jesus depicts love, and the Holy Spirit represents action.

Zoroastrians hold similar beliefs about the Amesha-Spentas. They say that the Sacred Seven represent aspects of God which are comparable to characteristics of men. The radiant energy dispersed through Ahura-Mazda is like light diffused through a spectrum, and the Holy Seven constitute this light. Or they may be compared to forces by and through which

God operates and manifests himself. Or, again, they constitute the ladder upon which man rises to absolute truth. They
may also be likened to fragments that, when assembled, are
a complete whole. Or, they may be compared to personalities
that, when unified, comprise the oneness of God, the oneness
of the universe, and the oneness of man.

The names and qualities of the Amesha-Spentas are clearly
defined in Zoroastrianism:

Ahura-Mazda .... *God the Eternal Light*
Asha   ....*Knowledge of Right and Justice*
Vohu Manah .... *Good Mind and Mind of Love*
·Kshathra .... *Strength of Spirit*
Armaiti .... *Piety and Faith*
Haurvatat .... *Health and Perfection*
Ameretat .. ..*Immortality*

Whenever Parsis mentioned the Holy Seven or the Holy
Heptad, they were thinking in terms of qualities of God. For
example, there are times in life when Asha must be called
upon—times when there is special need for a knowledge of
right and justice. Or there are moments when Armaiti, or the
qualities of piety and faith, are particularly needed. And
every man at one time or another surely thinks most particularly about Ameretat, or the meaning of immortality.

THE PLACE OF EVIL

But Zoroaster claimed that Ahura-Mazda and the Amesha-
Spentas were having no easy time of it, even as man him-
self had never found it easy or simple to live the good life.
Long before the apostle Paul gave his ideas on the subject,
Zoroaster recognized that when a man wished to do good,
something tempted him to do evil. What was this something?

How to explain this riddle—how to square the existence
of suffering and evil in the world with the good and gracious
Ahura-Mazda—was the question Zoroaster set out to solve.
Tradition says the answer came to him one evening as he
watched the sun go down. Lost in meditation, he beheld the
crimson afterglow change to gray, then grow deeper and
deeper until the blackness of night covered the earth. Even
nature, mused Zoroaster, is struggling. Night conquers day,
but then day again arises to conquer night. Evil conquers man,
but one day man conquers evil.

Surely, Zoroaster concluded, it must be that the great
Ahura-Mazda planned it this way. Since he gave man free
will, must he not also give man opposites from which to
choose? Light and darkness, good and evil, hope and despair
—it was up to man to make his choice. This was most certainly the answer.

> "One Spirit is good, the other bad;
> And of these two the wise will choose aright,
> The unwise choose not thus—and go astray."

So says the Avesta. And so was born, more than 2,500
years ago, the doctrine of duality—the belief that the universe is under the domination of two opposite principles.
Ahura-Mazda was recognized as the Creator not only of good
but also of evil. He was Lord not only of spirit but of matter.
He was God not only of truth but of falsehood. And his
purpose was to lead man by way of the Amesha-Spentas into
the fullness of the knowledge of God.

Ahura-Mazda—the name itself was a dual name, Zoroaster
explained. Not two gods but two gods in one. Life, to the
Zoroastrian and the Parsi, is, therefore, a school—a place
of learning and decision. Life is the lottery where man can
choose either the god of light or the god of darkness. The

purpose of life is the attainment of good, but this attainment is meaningful only if evil exists.

Soon Zoroaster began to say that the unseen world was inhabited by Seven Satans to match the Sacred Seven. He claimed that each good spirit in the Amesha-Spentas had its opponent just as each good intention of man has its counterpart of evil design. It worked like this: The evil counterpart of Ahura-Mazda was known as Angra Mainyu or Ahriman, the Prince of Darkness. Opposing holy Asha, who was Knowledge of Right, was the demon Druj, who signified Falsehood. Vohu Manah, the Good Mind, was opposed by Akem, or Evil Mind. Kshathra, known as Strength of Spirit, was challenged by Dush-Kshathra, or Cowardice. Armaiti, the Spirit of Piety and Faith, had as its countercreation Taromaiti, or False Pretense. Haurvatat—Health and Perfection—was contested by Avetat, or Misery; Ameretat, or Immortality, had as its opponent a devil named Merethyn, who signified Annihilation.

Parsis told me exactly what Zoroaster must have told the people of his time: "These representations do not mean that we worship many gods or that we are idolatrous. You will find no images in our homes or temples. We are monotheists. We worship the one true God, Ahura-Mazda. But we know that life is a struggle between good and evil, between the Sacred Seven and the Seven Satans. They are fighting for power in the world, and they are struggling for supremacy over our lives. We can join forces with either the Sacred Seven or the Seven Satans. It is up to us to make the choice."

To the Parsis the conflict between good and evil constitutes a law. All creation divides itself into that which is Ahura-Mazda's and that claimed by Angra Mainyu. According to Zoroaster the only way to find the good life and eventually redeem the world is by good thoughts, good words, and good deeds. To know, to love, to serve—these are the greatest truths.

This was the teaching Zoroaster brought to the world—a teaching that was neither simple nor easy to live. It asked men to put aside their images and begin living the good life. It meant a working philosophy rather than playing around with magical formulas as the early Magi had done. Indeed, for a time it seemed as though no one would ever willingly follow such a faith. But after ten years of preaching Zoroaster converted a cousin of his, and after several years more he convinced King Vishtaspa that Ahura-Mazda was superior in wisdom, spirit, and power to the gods of the palace priests.

THE AVESTA

Soon thereafter Zoroastrianism became a national faith, and from Persia its teachings went out into all the world in the form of the Avesta. This body of writing was penned, it is said, by the king's scribe under the inspiration and dictation of Zoroaster. It consists of many books, as does the Christian Bible, and it speaks beautifully and instructively on many phases of the life of man.

Of God's will it says, "He created all creatures for progress, which is his wish; and it is necessary for us to promote whatever is his wish that our wish may be realized."

Of marriage it states this viewpoint: "He that hath a wife is far above him that liveth in continence; he that maintaineth a household is far above him that hath none; he that hath children is far above him that hath no child."

Of healing it says: "He who heals with the Holy Word, this man is the best. He will best drive away sickness from the body of the one of the faith."

Concerning death and dying we find these words: "Up riseth Vohu-Manah from his golden throne. He will take the blessed one by the hand and make him rejoice as much as doth the man when on the pinnacle of nobility and glory."

Of the resurrection it says: "The dead shall rise. Life shall return to their bodies, and they shall breathe again."

And about the final judgment it says that there is a book of life in which man's divine qualities and man's sins are scrupulously listed. At the end of life the book is opened, and each person is judged at a tollgate on the "sifting bridge" that leads to heaven. If a man has a credit balance, he is escorted into paradise. If he is in moral debt to God, he goes to hell. If the credits and debits are equal, the soul goes to purgatory, there to await the final judgment.

A Parsi said to me, "Our faith and yours have much in common."

"Some say we owe Zoroaster a debt," I answered.

"Each owes a debt to the other," he replied.

"And what about the temple? Can I possibly go inside?" I asked.

My Parsi friend, prominent in Bombay, said I could. Was it as easy as that? Not ordinarily, he explained, but by a stroke of fate a certain temple was being renovated, and the holy fire had been moved into a separate enclosed room.

"The fire is holy," he said, "and no infidel eyes should defame it."

In this case I was the infidel. I was not a Parsi and was therefore outside the fold.

"Do you worship the fire?" I asked.

"The grossest error is to call us fire worshipers," he replied. "We do not worship it. It is a symbol—a symbol of the fire of God that burns in our hearts. Let it never go out. Let it never be defamed."

He told me that at Udvada, north of Bombay, a temple
fire had been burning uninterruptedly for one thousand years.
Only the most expensive wood—sandalwood—is used to feed
the flames.

It should be so with the divine fire in the human heart,
he explained. If the temple fire ever did go out, it would be
necessary, he said, to rekindle it from some other temple;
or, best of all, a person should get fire from God. He meant
finding a fire that lightning had kindled. That was virgin fire
—the fire of Ahura-Mazda—which Zoroaster carried from
temple to temple as places of worship were erected in his day.
That was the fire in front of which Zoroaster met his death
when he was assassinated by a Turanian while he prayed.

So we came to the temple. It was an unimpressive stone
building that might have been an old mansion or even a fac-
tory building in Bombay. An unpretentious doorway led
into a small open court, and here on a small bench in the
shadows sat a bearded priest who might have been Zoroaster
himself, considering his patriarchal seventy years.

Tall and smiling, he arose and shook my hand. Speaking
English, he said he was glad that I had come. He was right
about one thing. He said there was not much to see, and, indeed, this was true. The single large room was plain and
austere. It could have been a conservative, humble church
with several small adjoining rooms of the kind we would use
for Sunday-school classes. The aging, gray walls, the stark,
unadorned columns, and a pile of sandalwood cut into sticks
about a foot long were actually about all there was to see.

There was a closed-off room, however, and in it, I was
told, the fire burned. During services the fire is a prominent
feature of worship, for it also represents the sun, which
Persians, even before Zoroaster, worshiped in the Mithras
cult. "To fire," says the ritual, "special reverence is due be-

cause we owe to it the existence and sustenance of man."

Here in the temple the members of the Zoroastrian faith worship the spirits of holy men, invoke the Amesha-Spentas, read the Avesta, and, through prayers and chants, endeavor to fortify the good against the evil.

"What about the temple bull?" I asked my Parsi friend.

"Why, yes," he replied. Then he turned to the priest. "He may see it, may he not?"

My counterpart of Zoroaster nodded and smiled. Escorting us to a balustrade, he invited us to look down into a grassy court some thirty feet square. Here, tethered to a stake, was a huge white bull.

My friend anticipated my question. "It would not be right to say we worship him," he said. "He is a symbol."

"Of what?"

"Of God's creative and procreative power in the universe." The priest then explained that the animal was held in high esteem. Did I notice that there was not a black or gray hair on it? It required long and ardent searching to find him.

The urine of the bull is sacred. Blessed by priests in a special ceremony, it actually undergoes a chemical change, I was told. Drops of it are used for special religious ceremonies.

RITUALS FOR THE DEAD

Neither the priest nor my friend saw anything incongruous in the manner in which the Parsis dispose of their dead. Why should they? Did not the Avesta prescribe how and why these things should be done?

"Two men," say the scriptures, "strong and agile, having changed their garments, shall lift the body from the clay or from the stones, or out of the plastered house, and they shall lay it down at a place where they know that there are always corpse-eating dogs and corpse-eating birds."

The earth, being sacred, should not be contaminated with the dead. Fire, being holy, should not be defiled by a corpse. A dead body, being the natural abode for the devils of disease and contagion, had best be consumed by the beasts or the birds.

There was something else. There was another viewpoint about giving one's body to the scavengers to consume. It was explained to me calmly but forcibly as I stood with my friend in the shadow of the Tower of Silence. This lofty structure, looking like a deserted campanile, stood hauntingly alone at the edge of the city. On its truncated roof were stone slabs upon which dead bodies could be placed, and openings between the slabs permitted the bones to drop into a subterranean cave after the flesh had been devoured.

We stood looking silently toward the structure. There were no bodies there, but the black vultures soared above the tower just the same. It was then my friend explained to me his point of view.

"We Parsis feel," he said thoughtfully, "that giving our bodies to God's creatures is our final act of charity."

I shall never forget that. It is one thing for a believer to take you into his temple of worship. It is an even greater privilege to be taken into the temple of his heart.

But, then, why shouldn't he? Is it not written in his scriptures that the Amesha-Spentas look into one another's souls and meditate upon good thoughts, good words, and good deeds? And do they not also think upon Paradise, whose way is good and whose path through heaven shines with glory?

So says the Avesta, and so say the Parsis, who love and respect one of the world's oldest and most venerable prophets —Zoroaster, the Persian seer.

Glossary

Chapter 4: Buddhistic Terms *

Bodhi (bō'dĭ) Enlightenment.

Bodhisattva (bō'dĭ-săt'wà) A person who has started on the path of Buddhahood and who, generally in a future incarnation, will become a Buddha.

Buddha (bōŏd'à) The name given an incarnation of self-abnegation, virtue, and wisdom.

Buddhism (bōŏd'ĭz'm) The religion based upon the doctrine first taught by Gautama Buddha. His main revelation consisted in a perception of the causes of suffering and the way in which salvation from suffering can be achieved.

Maya (mā'yä) The mother of Buddha.

nirvana (nĭr-vä'nà) The final extinction, in the heart, of the threefold fire of passion, hatred, and delusion. This process involves a blessed spiritual condition.

Pitaka (pĭt'à·kà) One of the three divisions of the Buddhist Scriptures.

stupa (stōō'pà) A Buddhist mound, which forms a memorial shrine of the Buddha.

Tripitaka (trĕ·pĭt'à·kà) The three divisions of Buddhist Scriptures.

---

* Many of the words used in this book are peculiar to the particular faiths or religions discussed. For this reason they may not be familiar to the average reader. Because these words are basic to an adequate understanding of these faiths, brief definitions have been provided at the outset of each discussion.

4

Buddhism
Religion of the Eightfold Path

I T IS one thing to learn about Buddhism in Western class-
rooms and quite another to hear it whispered in your ear
by a scholarly, bespectacled Asiatic of forty who loves his
lord, the Lord Buddha. This was my experience at Sarnath,
India, where the Buddha preached his first sermon nearly
2,500 years ago.

A PRINCE WHO BECAME A BEGGAR

There is a rare and beautiful museum in the tiny, dreamy
village of Sarnath. There are also ruins of old Buddhist monasteries, and there is a temple for prayer. But most fascinating are the murals in the headquarters building depicting
scenes from the life of Gautama Buddha, the prince who became a beggar for the sake of God. It was here at the murals
that my companion confided his remarks to me in a softly
animated voice, while groups of people from many lands
stood around us, also looking up at the life-sized paintings.
The Buddha's name is holy throughout Asia, and it is said
that among the 150,000,000 members of the faith around the
world eighty thousand are Americans.

Buddhists truly believe that their master, the Buddha, descended from heaven to save mankind. The murals depicted the soul of the Buddha as living in heaven where he was one with God since the beginning of time. There he awaited the hour he should be revealed to men. That day, according to Buddhists, came in 563 B.C. The Buddhistic soul, called the Bodhisattva, left its heavenly home to assume the form and nature of man.

The picture story is here at Sarnath for all the world to see. It depicts the miraculous birth for which God had selected Queen Maha Maya, wife of King Sudhodanna Gautama of the Sakya tribe in the Himalayan valley of the Ganges. It portrays the annunciation and the birth of the child in the Lumbini gardens and tells of the prediction of the king's soothsayers that this first-born son, Siddhartha Gautama, would abandon his right to the throne if ever he became acquainted with the suffering in the world.

Tradition has it that King Sudhodanna commanded his people, "Never let the eyes of my son behold either sorrow or death." And in the palace grounds Prince Gautama saw only the apparent happiness of his father's court. In his journeys to the cities couriers preceded him so that nothing in the form of sadness should ever mar his path. For thirty years Prince Siddhartha Gautama lived in a make-believe world, enjoying a kind of make-believe peace.

Because there were miracles during this sheltered existence, the murals at Sarnath told the stories of these, too. Tenderly they recorded how the young prince fell asleep in the shade of a tree and how, though the shade of every other tree shifted with the sun, the prince's tree remained constant in deference to the holy child.

, At the age of twelve the prince astounded his teachers with his superior knowledge. At sixteen he so distinguished himself at archery that he won the right to marry his cousin, Yasodhara, a girl who, it is said, was born on the same day of his birth.

"Legends," affirmed my companion, but all these things were true to him in substance. There is meaning behind the myths, he said, and the meaning is known to Buddhists whether they worship in the gold-covered temple of the Shwe Dagon in Burma or in the decaying stupas along the Ganges, where my companion had his home. The mythical touch has a mystical quality, he declared, and I could see that it all meant very much to him.

SUFFERING AND SADNESS

Then the murals showed how, at the age of thirty, Prince Gautama was suddenly confronted full force with life's realities. Although the couriers had carefully prepared the route, there appeared in the prince's path an old man sorrowfully trudging his burdened way along the road. A bit farther on, a sick man huddled, bowed down with disease. And finally, amid the mourners' cries, the prince beheld a corpse that was being carried to the waiting funeral pyre.

These three scenes, my companion assured me, were staged by the gods to acquaint Prince Gautama with the tragedy of age, suffering, and the sorrow of death, from one or all of which no living soul is spared.

The divinely human drama plunged Siddhartha Gautama into deep sadness. He could never forget what he had seen, nor could he ever erase from his mind the contrast which he observed in a serene and peaceful monk reflectively walking the same highway of life. Surely the religious man had found the answer to life's riddles. Surely the man who set his heart on God would find peace.

DIVINITY IN EVERY MAN

Haunted by his thoughts Siddhartha made his choice. His final decision was one that Christians would find difficult to understand or justify, for the prince abandoned his son, Rahaula, and his wife, whom he dearly loved, and fled from his father's house at night in a search for God. While Christians might call it desertion, Buddhists refer to it reverently as "the night of the great renunciation."

I had a question. "Was Siddhartha Gautama aware of his divinity during these years?"

My friend replied, "Is not every man aware of it—at times?"

This was the heart of it. There is divinity in every man. Every man is a Bodhisattva—one who bears within himself the immortal essence. My companion believed that it was a great lesson. Is not the Buddha's life the legend of every man?

We, too, have been born in a palace—the palace of God, our King. We, too, came into the world bearing in our hearts God's likeness. Protected for a time from the full impact of the world, we are never quite spurred to thought about our destiny and the meaning of life until we see, as did Prince Gautama, suffering, old age, and death. Then we begin to wonder about life. We look about us, and we also see the holy man walking. We see him who has set his heart on God and who has come to terms with a spiritual philosophy. The man of God is the most serene, the best adjusted, the most perfectly equipped to master life. His happiness is an inward happiness; his strength is an inner strength.

Behind the legend was the truth as the Buddha himself expresses it in one of the holy writings: "O disciples, in my father's mansion there was a pond with lotus flowers. My room was always perfumed . . . my clothes were made of the finest cloth. Whenever I went out, I was sheltered with a white umbrella. I had a winter house in winter, a summer house in summer, and a spring house in spring. During the four months of rainy season, women played music for me. O disciples, though I was thus happy and wealthy, I happened to think, 'A foolish mediocrity grows old, and [man] cannot escape growing old. . . . A foolish mediocrity becomes sick, and [man] cannot escape becoming sick. . . . A foolish mediocrity dies, and [man] cannot escape death. And yet he loathes the dead. I also am destined to die, and I do not know how to escape death. It is not proper for me to loathe to see others die while I am also to die some day.' O disciples, when I observed thus, all the pride I took in my life left me."

SEEKING A REASON FOR SUFFERING

Having left his father's house, the Buddha was sorely tempted. Gods, disguised as devils, offered him the kingdoms of the earth if only he would bow down and serve them. He fasted and prayed. He fasted so strenuously that he often fell into a dead faint. His five disciples, who knew him only as a seeker like themselves, were convinced he was especially holy because he mortified his body more than they. But one day the wandering Siddhartha said to them, "Starving myself and torturing myself is bringing me no nearer the answers to my questions than when I lived in ease and pleasure in my father's house!"

That, declared my companion, was a human cry. It is the cry of every man who seeks the cause of suffering, who finds that every supreme happiness is accompanied by suffering, and who tries to reconcile suffering with a merciful God. A man is tempted to return home as Siddhartha was. A man is deserted by his friends as the disciples deserted Gautama. But there are also men who continue the quest, as the Bodhisattva did, and such a man is inevitably led to the bodhi tree.

The bodhi tree was symbolized in the murals as the tree of knowledge. This particular one was depicted as a fig tree and stood at Gaya of Magadha in north India. Here, beneath this tree, Siddhartha Gautama sat. He was determined not to rise until he had solved the riddle of suffering and pain. Like Jacob wrestling with the angel, he said he would never let God go until God had blessed him. And here, at midnight during the seventh week, beneath the sacred tree whose branches are in heaven and whose roots clutch the heart of the earth, he received his illumination.

And what did that mean? It meant that he had discovered a series of truths. He "relived the endless cycles of cause and effect within the universe." He had reached a conclusion: "From good must always come good, and from evil, evil."

This illumination had come from a retracing of his steps back to heaven from whence he came, where, from the beginning of time, he had been with God. Now Gautama realized anew what Hinduism had always taught: "The true self is God, and God is the true self." Finally, he had found the answer to the question of suffering which he was later to expound here at Sarnath.

The truth of the matter was this: A man had come to the tree of knowledge as a pilgrim; he arose as the Buddha—the Enlightened One; and the time of his transfiguration is referred to by his followers as the "Sacred Night."

Gautama's disciples returned to him. They came to scoff because they were unable to believe that a man who had rejected extreme asceticism, just as he had earlier renounced extreme happiness, could ever find enduring peace. They came here to Sarnath, to the Deer Park called Isipatana. As

my companion told me this story, he seemed to see them as
clearly in his mind as I saw them illustrated on the walls.
They came to scoff, but they remained to kneel at the feet of
the Blessed One.

FOUR GREAT TRUTHS

The sermon the Buddha preached at Sarnath is called "Setting in Motion the Wheel of the Law," and the heart of it is
the riddle and solution of suffering based on four noble
truths: (1) the truth of suffering; (2) the cause of suffering;
(3) the cessation of suffering; (4) the way that leads to the
cessation of suffering.

"Hear, O my disciples," said the Buddha, "this is the
noble truth of suffering: Birth is suffering; old age is suffer-
ing; sickness is suffering; death is suffering; sorrow, lamenta-
tion, dejection, and despair are suffering. Contact with un-
pleasant things is suffering. . . . And this is the cause of
suffering: the craving thirst, which tends to rebirth, com-
bined with pleasure and lust, finding pleasure here and there;
namely, the craving for passion, the craving for existence,
the craving for vanity. . . . Now, the cessation of suffering is
to cease from attachment. Attachment originates in craving,
and craving originates in ignorance. To cease from suffering,
cease from attachment; to cease from attachment, cease from
craving; to cease from craving, cease from ignorance. . . .
And now, my disciples, the noble truth of the *way* that leads
to cessation of suffering is the noble eightfold path, namely:
right views, right intention, right speech, right action, right
livelihood, right effort, right mindfulness, right concentration."

So great was the appeal not only of his words but of his
logic and his life that young men and women began flocking

to Sarnath, drawn by the light of the Enlightened One. The
people of nearby Benares complained that the Buddha was
robbing the city of its youth. He answered them by saying he
had come to turn men's hearts from fruitless speculation to
an awareness of truth. He had come to teach the cause and
cure of suffering, to lift men above their pettinesses, to dis-
tinguish between reality and illusion. His way was uniquely
devoid of talk about God or gods; he had little to say about
prophecy, less to say about worship, and even less about the
deification of himself.

Statues of the Buddha are now found in almost every part
of the world. There are golden ones that are truly works of
art, and before many of these images the faithful prostrate
themselves. There are also relics connected with Buddha and
shrines for housing these. Even Buddha's tooth is venerated
and held as sacrosanct. The records state, however, that the
Buddha is said to have explained at Sarnath, "If you try to
see me through my form, or if you try to hear me through my
voice, you will never reach me."

LOVE AND DISCIPLINE

Although leaders like Asoka in Magadha, India, and his
son Mahinda in Ceylon ambitiously propagated the faith
and built temples, monasteries, and nunneries, and although
they worshiped the bodhi tree, such was hardly the Buddha's
plan. He declared, "One act of pure love in saving life is
greater than spending the whole of one's time in religious
offerings to the gods."

Though there are sects within sects all the way from
Lamaism in Tibet to Hinayana (Theravada) in Asia and Cey-
on and Mahayana in China, this was not the Buddha's wish.
Though there are a formalistic Tendai School of Buddhism,

a mystical Shingon School, the renowned Pure Land School, the Zen School, and many others, the Buddha simply said, "Let your light so shine before the world that you, having embraced the religious life according to our well-taught doctrine and discipline, may be seen by men as possessing forbearance and meekness."

Because he said that God could not be limited, described, defined, or explained, many said that the Buddha was an atheist. He said simply that God is and that this is the sum and substance of his Being. The Buddha did not deny the existence of God; he contended that God's existence is beyond understanding, above definition, and outside the grasp of God himself. God does not know what he is, because he is not any *what*. He does not know who he is, because he is not any *who*. He is beyond desire, craving, wanting, wishing, and beyond such unrealities as age, suffering, death. And when a man has entered that condition—when he, too, is above both existence and nonexistence—he is lost in God. He is in nirvana.

Unlike Hinduism, the faith of the Buddha was beyond the concept of caste. Like Christianity, Buddhism is no respecter of persons. "My doctrine," said the Enlightened One, "makes no distinction between high and low or between rich and poor. It is like the sky. It has room for all; and like the rain, it washes all alike."

The visitors to Sarnath moved past us. A group of Roman Catholic nuns paused as if listening to my companion as he spoke. Did they know, I wondered, that Jerome compared the Buddha's life to that of Christ and that the legend of Josaphat is the story of the Bodhisattva?

Glorious was the story of how King Sudhodanna and the Buddha's wife and son united with the faith, and glorious were the legends that the holy name of the Buddha wrought.

Judging from the way his death was portrayed by the murals and described by my interpreter as we stood in those Sarnath halls, even this part of the Buddha's experience must have been glorious.

"In a grove of trees the seventy-five-year-old Buddha called his beloved disciple Ananda and told him not to weep. Whatever is born bears within itself the seed of dissolution. And to all of his disciples he said, 'Impermanent are compound things. Work out your salvation with earnestness.'"

The Pitakas

Buddha's followers gathered his sayings, his teachings, and his philosophy into holy books called Pitakas. The Sanskrit word means "baskets" and applies especially to the containers in which archaeologists reverently store their findings through their years of searching and sifting for the secrets of man's life on earth. Buddhism's sacred canon contains three baskets called Tipitaka or Tripitaka. They urged Buddha's followers to do good and offered to them a golden rule that said, "Hurt not others with that which pains yourself." They also spoke of ten commandments that said:

1. Thou shalt not kill.
2. Thou shalt not steal.
3. Thou shalt not commit adultery.
4. Thou shalt not be deceitful.
5. Thou shalt not curse.
6. Thou shalt not lie.
7. Thou shalt not speak vanity.
8. Thou shalt not covet.
9. Thou shalt not insult or flatter.
10. Thou shalt be free from anger and revenge.

The teaching had a challenge that closely resembles our
Great Commission (Matthew 28:19-20) and which commanded, "Go now, O monks, and wander for the benefit of
the many, for the welfare of mankind, out of compassion for
the world. Preach the doctrine. If it is not preached to them,
they cannot attain salvation. Proclaim to them a life of holiness."

"And as the Blessed One had set going the Wheel of the
Law," say the holy Buddhistic scriptures, "the earth-inhabit-
ing gods shouted, 'Truly the Blessed One has set going in
the Deer Park, Isipatana, the Wheel of the Law, which may
not be opposed by any being in the world.' Thus in that
moment, in that instant, in that second, the shout reached the
Brahma world; and this whole system of ten thousand worlds
quaked, was shaken and trembled; and an infinite, mighty
light was seen throughout the world."

What else was there to say? Quietly I went with my companion into the out-of-doors, past the huge temple gong,
past the groups of people, and out among the sacred ruins.
Perhaps it was here the Buddha walked or here the Buddha
stood as he preached to those who were eager to hear. It
may have been that he sat here on this hill or meditated in
this valley. Who could say?

In those golden days at Sarnath when he ruled by example
and spoke in truth, his disciples asked, "Tell us, Enlightened
One, wherein does religion consist?"

He answered them, "It consists in doing as little harm
as possible, in doing good in abundance, in the practice of
love, compassion, truthfulness, and purity in all walks of
life."

And they said to him, "But tell us, then, where is heaven?"

He replied, "You have already found it when you walk the
eightfold path: right views, right intention, right speech, right

action, right livelihood, right effort, right mindfulness, right concentration."

So says Buddhism today, and so said my companion. And both would add that the Buddha's thoughts are right because they are reasonable, and reasonable because they are right.

Glossary

CHAPTER 5: JUDAISTIC TERMS *

Diaspora (dĭ·ăs'pô·rà) Jews, who, after the Babylonian captivity, were scattered throughout the Old World.

Gemarah (gĕ·mä'rä) The commentary based on the Mishnah.

Hanukkah (hä'nŏŏ·kä) The Jewish Feast of Dedication, which celebrates the Maccabean victory over the Greeks.

Judaism (jōō'dà·ĭz'm) The religious doctrines of Jews. It may also refer to the Jewish religious system in general.

Midrash (mĭd'răsh) An exposition of the Hebrew Scriptures or a part of them.

Mishnah (mĭsh'nà) Traditional Jewish doctrine as it developed by means of the decisions of rabbis before the third century A.D.

Passover (pàs'ō'vĕr) An annual feast of the Jews commemorating the sparing of the Hebrews in Egypt when the first-born of the Egyptians were slain.

Pentateuch (pĕn'tà·tūk) The first five books of the Old Testament.

Pentecost (pĕn'tĕ·kŏst) A solemn Jewish festival observed on the fiftieth day (seven weeks) after the second day of Passover.

Purim (pū'rĭm) A Jewish feast commemorating Esther's intervention on behalf of the Jews in Persia.

Rosh Hashana (rōsh hä·shä'nä) The Jewish New Year.

Seder (sä'dĕr) A festival held in Jewish homes on the first night of Passover. Its chief purpose is to commemorate the Exodus from Egypt.

---

* Many of the words used in this book are peculiar to the particular faiths or religions discussed. For this reason they may not be familiar to the average reader. Because these words are basic to an adequate understanding of these faiths, brief definitions have been provided at the outset of each discussion.

Shabuoth (shă·vōō'ōth) The Jewish festival that is also called the Feast of Weeks (Pentecost).

Sukkoth (sŏŏk·ōth') The Jewish Feast of Tabernacles, a harvest festival.

Talmud (tăl'mŭd) Jewish civil and canonical law as it has been preserved by Jews. It consists of the Mishnah and the Gemara.

Thummim (thŭm'ĭm) The Urim (see below) and Thummim were certain objects mentioned in the Old Testament which were used as means to reveal God's will to his people. On certain occasions high priests wore them in their breastplates.

Torah (tō'rā) The Pentateuch, or Law of Moses.

Urim (ū'rĭm) (See *Thummim* above.)

Yahweh (yā'wĕ) A transliteration of the Hebrew word for Jehovah.

Yom Kippur (yōm kĭp'ŏŏr) The Jewish Day of Atonement.

Zionism (zī'ŭn·ĭz'm) Among modern Jews this term refers to a movement for colonizing Jews in Palestine.

Zohar (zō'hăr) A Jewish cabalistic book written in the form of a commentary on the Pentateuch.

5

Judaism
Religion of a Divine Destiny

ONE summer afternoon I walked into the new state of
Israel through the only accessible corridor—the Mandelbaum Gate. The narrow, three-hundred-foot-long passage
was a barricaded lane, guarded at one end by Arab legion-
naires and at the other by Israeli soldiers. They were armed
with "Tommy guns," and during recent days there had been
a number of border incidents. Special permission had been
granted me to cross.

On the Israeli side, a member of the border patrol asked
me my business. When I informed him that my work was in
the field of religion, he showed great interest.

"You have come to a good place," he said. "This is the
Lord's land."

He may have meant the territory over which the blue-and-
white-striped flag with the imprint of the Star of David was
flying, or he may have been referring to the area on both
sides of the formidable Mandelbaum Gate. The Republic of
Israel occupies the major portion of Palestine, but all of this
country is holy land in the sense that it is holy to Jew, Christian, and Moslem. The oldest traditions belong to the Jews.
The oldest landmarks are Jewish, as are also the oldest cere-

61

monial observances. The Sabbath, the Day of Atonement, the Festival of Passover, the Feast of Booths or Tabernacles, and Pentecost are part of the heritage of the Hebrew people.

JUDAISM TODAY

All of the "Lord's land"—bountifully rich in tradition and religious lore—is intricately linked with Judaism, the faith of some twelve million people, about six million of whom live in the United States, and nearly two million of whom now claim citizenship in Israel.

As I made my way to the King David Hotel in the more modern section of Jerusalem (old Jerusalem is in the Arab sector), I saw bearded, patriarchal-looking Jews everywhere along the way. They were rugged and ruddy-cheeked. Dressed in black suits and wearing rather broad-brimmed black hats, they greatly resembled our Amish people in Pennsylvania. I saw them in the midst of the moving traffic, and when I contrasted them with the modern young Israelis who were dressed as though they had just stepped from the sidewalks of New York, I realized again how diverse and fabulous is the history of this faith, especially when seen through its people in the holy land of Zion.

A CHOSEN PEOPLE

Judaism's entrance into the pageantry of sacred history was highly dramatic. The first five books of Moses, called the Pentateuch, tell the story, and it is a saga going back at least three thousand years. Christians, no less than Jews, thrill at the majesty of words familiar to every participant in the Judaeo-Christian tradition. "In the beginning God created the heavens and the earth. . . . God created man in his own image, in the image of God he created him; male and female he created them. And God blessed them . . . . And God saw everything that he had made, and behold, it was very good." (Genesis 1:1, 27-28, 31.)

Other books of the Old Testament continue the unfoldment, prophecies, beliefs, sufferings, and aspirations of the people of Israel. We see them as nomads wandering in the desert, as slaves serving the Pharaohs, and as free men liberated by the great God Yahweh. From places to which they have been dispersed they have come to forge a new nation against tremendous odds. In all these situations we behold them in a spectacular drama.

The miracle being performed in the Israeli republic is in keeping with the historic manifestations with which Judaism is replete: the flight from Egypt, the crossing of the Red Sea, the wanderings in the wilderness. Every traveler in Israel—regardless of his views about the political implications, the rightness or wrongness of the Arab-Israeli dispute, or his feeling about Zionism—cannot help being impressed by the spiritual fervor uniting and undergirding this achievement. Sharp religious, social, and political differences among the people are sublimated in an age-old saying, "Israel chose Yahweh to be their God, and Yahweh chose Israel to be his people."

This is the heart of the thinking of these people and to be mindful of this fact is to know Judaism. These people are convinced that God recognized, selected, and prepared them to be his chosen ones. They feel that he chose them not for special privileges but for special service and a special mission in his world. They believe that somewhere in "the Lord's land" the meaning behind the miracles lies fully revealed. Somewhere among the wastelands Yahweh's mountain holds the secret as to how and when the finger of God wrote the

Ten Commandments. Somewhere Abraham entertained angels unawares. Somewhere on Mount Carmel Elijah confounded and conquered the priests of Baal. Somewhere Saul was anointed king, David sang his psalms, Solomon built his Temple. Somewhere Isaiah prophesied about the coming of a Savior, Immanuel. All this is Judaism and its heritage. From earliest Hebrew history to the forging of the state of Israel, Judaism is the religion of a divine destiny.

It is this sense of destiny which unites the Hebrews although they are still a scattered people. From the most obscure Jew to the head of the Israeli republic and from the youngest Jewish child to the oldest rabbi the feeling of God's patronage is a driving force.

The Hebrews believe that is not an easy way that Yahweh has prepared. There will be persecution for righteousness' sake. Also, they feel that it is not a clearly marked path over which they must go, because God hides his purposes even as he hid himself from Moses on Sinai. Further, it is not a journey without crisis; Jehovah has his way of testing his children. But about his advocacy there can be no question.

THE TORAH

Inherent in the destiny of Judaism is the Torah, the sacred scroll. It holds a central place in every synagogue, is read at every Sabbath service, and is dear to the heart of every Israelite. Torah means "the law" and is regarded as the Jewish Bible. It also forms part of our Old Testament, but it is more meaningful for the Jew than for the Gentile. Enshrined in it is the revealed will of God, and upon it Judaism bases its code and conduct.

The Torah contains the awesome identification of Yahweh which is set forth in the emblazoned words, "I AM WHO I

AM" (Exodus 3:14). Here, too, is the supreme pronounce-
ment that has made Judaism foremost among the monothe-
istic faiths of ancient days, "Hear, O Israel: The LORD our
God is one LORD . . ." (Deuteronomy 6:4). The Torah is the
treasury of hope and assurance, the direct line of communication between a people and their God. For the Hebrews, Torah
is the Word, and the Word is Torah. It is the entire body of
doctrine and Scripture to which the Jew is bound and through
which he is freed from superstition and groundless fear. The
Torah is Judaism, and, as part of the divine destiny, it unites
the people wherever the Star of David stands. In Judaism,
particularly, the holy Scriptures have much significance.

THE TALMUD AND OTHER SACRED WRITINGS

Judaism is also the Talmud. Just as the Torah is the written law of the chosen people, so the Talmud was once the
oral law. Now codified, it has brought together the Mishnah
and the Gemarah (rabbinical studies) and interprets, illus-
trates, and amplifies the written law. The Talmud is the oral
Torah in which the immortal men of the synagogue have
pooled their wisdom and their revelations. In it Simon the
Just declares, "The world is established on three things: on
law, on worship, and on generosity."

In the Talmud we also find Rabbi Hillel's words, "More
flesh, more worms; more wealth, more worry; more women,
more witchcraft; more concubines, more lechery; more slaves,
more thievery. But more law, more life; more study, more
wisdom; more counsel, more clarity; more righteousness,
more peace." In it the wise teacher Akabya ben Mahalalel
advises, "Keep three things in mind, and you will escape the
toils of wickedness: Know whence you have come, whither

you are going, and before whom you will have to give a strict
account of yourself."

Instruction and counsel are also found in the Midrash,
which probes the biblical texts so that God's required guidance may be clear. Mysticism and its speculations are found
in the Zohar, the book which is the text for cabalistic seekers
after hidden truths. These persons search their holy writings
for the answers to such questions as, What is the soul of
man? How can good and evil be distinguished? What is the
nature of God? Is there a heaven and a hell? What is the
order of angels and demons? Throughout the history of the
wandering race these are questions that men who were called
"cabalists" weighed and pondered, dissecting every line, word,
and letter of the law to sound the secret depths.

SUFFERING AND DISPLACED PEOPLE

Judaism's destiny is also related to suffering and the remembrance of suffering. I realized this anew in Israel whenever citizens of the new state asked, "How are things over
there?" They were referring to conditions in old Jerusalem—
old Jerusalem where many shrines dear to their hearts are
sealed in Arab hands. Arabs later interrogated me about the
condition of things in Israel. There is longing and loneliness
for sacred places on both sides of the harrowing Mandelbaum Gate, but to no one more than the Jew does Jerusalem
mean the dwelling place of Yahweh.

Jerusalem has changed hands some forty times since David
made it the sanctuary for the ark of God. And today, as in
the days when Roman armies held the city shortly after the
Christian Era, Jews are forbidden to enter old Jerusalem and
mourn where their fathers mourned or die where their fathers
longed to die.

The sorrow of the Diaspora could have defeated Judaism, for, more than any other religious group, the Jews are a scattered and a separated people. It is easy to feel that assimilation might have absorbed them, for Jews have been forced to identify themselves with the cultures and languages of nations everywhere. Persecution made its repeated threat to stamp them out. From the ghetto to the gas chambers their oppression has been unmatched and the mass atrocities against them unparalleled. Judaism may seem symbolic of suffering and the remembrance of suffering, but we must remember that it also rests upon the principle that throughout all suffering a divine destiny shapes its course and guarantees its survival. Whatever men do to confound the Jewish people consistently unites them and crystallizes their culture into its unique and unconquerable form.

Holy Days

Judaism is also festivals and holy days descriptive of both sorrow and joy. The fabric of Judaic faith is woven on the loom of ceremonial observances. Many Christians are beginning to study the meaning of the Jewish Seder, the supper observed in connection with the Passover. It has a close historic and mystical relationship with the Lord's Supper, which is observed by Christians. Every Jewish child loves, honors, and respects the Seder. He knows its meaning. He never forgets how he sat with his parents around the Seder table and how, in the spell of tradition, he asked, "Why is this night different from all other nights?" And he remembers how his father answered, "We were slaves unto Pharaoh in Egypt, and the Eternal our God led us from there with a mighty hand."

Rosh Hashana, the Jewish New Year, coming in September or October according to the variations in the Jewish calendar, is a day of thoughtful soul searching.

Yom Kippur, the Day of Atonement, comes ten days after Rosh Hashanah and is a period of solemn rest. It is devoted to confession of sins, repentance, and reconciliation with God. Yom Kippur is a kind of Sabbath of Sabbaths. The Sabbath itself, which begins at dusk each Friday, is rigorously observed in Israel—more so, perhaps, than elsewhere because of the large number of Orthodox Jews. Orthodoxy forbids work on the Sabbath, fighting on the Sabbath, and travel on the Sabbath. Orthodoxy all over the world holds the Sabbath as an especially holy day of rest, and all Jews who follow their faith tend to honor the day from sundown to sundown.

Hanukkah, the Feast of Dedication, celebrates the Maccabean victory over the Greeks who had sought to Grecianize the Jews in the second century B.C. Judas Maccabeus "cleansed the temple" which the Greeks and Syrians had defiled. Purim is another festival of deliverance based on the story recorded in the Book of Esther.

Shabuoth is the Feast of Weeks, or feast of the first fruits of the harvest. It is also called Pentecost, which means literally "fifty days" after Passover.

Sukkoth, the Feast of Tabernacles or Booths, commemorates the ingathering of the harvest.

Deep within each festival is the insistent reminder that Judaism has endured much, has been delivered often, and has been consistently saved from absorption by the providence of God. Early in its history the influence of Zoroastrianism challenged it with its concept of dualism, but Judaism contended that God could not create an evil one coequal with himself. Buddhism might have transformed the Jewish Decalogue into a mere moral and ethical philosophy if the Jews had not insisted that Yahweh had directly transmitted the

words to them for a divine purpose even beyond their know-
ing. The Hindu belief in karma and reincarnation and castes
could have changed Judaism's views about the purpose of
life had it not been for the Jewish conviction that God's passion and desire is for social justice.

Though Judaism had connections with all these faiths,
it would not allow itself to be conquered. Instead, it incor-
porated whatever seemed to serve God's plan for the Jews
as children of his destiny. By a rare genius it created a religion without a specific dogma and a movement without a
specific founder save "the Eternal our God," who, in a very
real sense, has been made the Founder of the Hebrew state
of Israel, watching over his people.

JUDAISM AND CHRISTIANITY

As I walked Israeli streets and roamed the countryside of
this semidesert region, which is more and more becoming a
fertile plain, I thought of the many expressions in Hebrew
tradition which are part of the treasury of Christian thought.
There came to my mind phrases such as "the Promised
Land," "Lord God of hosts," "children of God," "the Mizpah
benediction," and many more. National groups, too, like
the Canaanites, Philistines, and Chaldeans, and tribes like
Ephraim and Manasseh and the other ten tribes leaped to
my attention. Gods like Moloch, Baal, and Beelzebub, all
named in the Scriptures, are intermingled in the Judaeo-
Christian tradition together with a wide range of theological
concepts. Often I stopped abruptly in my thoughts, realizing
that the main point of departure between us Christians and
the Jews is that we feel that the Messiah has come in Christ,
while they still await the advent of their promised one, Immanuel. And, especially, there is the cross!

This hope for his coming unites the Jewish people, too. This waiting and watching is a vital part of Judaism. When it is said that Moses received the law on Mount Sinai and handed it down to Joshua, who passed it on to the judges, who handed it down to the prophets, who give it to the men of the synagogues, it is implied that the hope of a deliverer was also handed down. He is to be the fulfillment of the law. To most Jews, the messianic hope remains a fundamental one.

BASIC CONCEPTS

To most Jews, too, there are also basic concepts that he must believe. Maimonides (Rabbi Moses ben Maimon), the foremost Talmudist of the Middle Ages, listed thirteen articles of belief based on the following subjects:

1. The existence of God
2. The unity of God
3. The spiritual nature of God
4. God's uniqueness in that he has always existed and will continue to exist forever
5. Worship of God
6. Prophecy
7. Moses as the greatest of prophets
8. The heavenly origin of the Law
9. The eternal nature of the Law
10. God's knowledge of the works of men
11. Reward and punishment
12. The coming of the Messiah
13. The resurrection of the dead

Other authorities had other interpretations. Among them was the scholar Hasdai Crescas, who, in the fifteenth century, listed fourteen points for Judaism's spiritual course:

1. God knows individually all things and all people.

2. His providence is over each individual.
3. He is omnipotent.
4. He revealed himself in a special way to the
   prophets.
5. He has given man freedom of the will.
6. He gave man the Torah.
> 7. He created the universe at a particular time.
8. Immortality is assured for those who observe his
   commandments.
9. There is punishment for the wicked.
10. The dead will be resurrected.
11. The Torah is eternal.
12. Moses is supreme.
13. The priest can foretell future events through the
    Urim and Thummim (objects mentioned in
    Exodus 28:30).
14. The Messiah will come.

Types of Judaism

Beliefs according to Maimonides, Crescas, or other fathers
of the faith down through the ages constitute the nature and
life of the Hebrew people and make the state of Israel the
center of Judaism as well as a homeland for the Jew. For
here in the Palestinian republic are represented the three
major types of Judaism—types that are also representative
of the American Jewish community. They are Orthodox
Judaism, Reform Judaism, and Conservative Judaism.

Orthodox Judaism represents an attempt to hold to tradi-
tionalism and ancient authority and is somewhat comparable
to fundamentalism in Protestantism. Reform Judaism, the
liberal or progressive movement, is comparable to liberal
Protestantism. And Conservative Judaism, the middle-of-the-
road Judaic expression, is comparable, perhaps, to liberal con-
servatism in the Protestant faith. Some 40 per cent of Amer-

ica's "practicing" Jews are Orthodox; 30 per cent are Reform, and 30 per cent are Conservative.

But more significant even than synagogue affiliation is the Jewish consciousness, molded through centuries of emphatic faith. Jews everywhere, wherever they may be and in whatever culture they are found, believe that they must worship God in the sanctuary of their hearts, for God has laid upon them a heritage that dare not be denied. They are of all nations, yet they are distinctive among the nations. They are noted for their keen business acumen, yet they are among the most philanthropic people. They are rationalistic, yet mystical. They are a people of intensive action, yet they rightly claim some of religion's most reflective scholars. Being divided even on Zionism and yet convinced that Jerusalem is their rightful home, they can best be understood by walking the age-old streets of their new nation. Here, in this tiny stronghold that is 120 miles long and 15 miles wide, amid modern innovations and a completely realistic outlook upon the world, is heard once more in the light of our time the ancient words, "Israel chose Yahweh to be their God, and Yahweh chose Israel to be his people."

Glossary

Chapter 6: Confucianistic and Taoistic Terms *

Analects (ăn'ȧ·lĕkts) A collection of literary passages attributed to Confucius.

Confucianism (kŏn·fū'shăn·ĭz'm) The ethics taught by Confucius and his disciples. It emphasizes filial piety, justice, propriety, benevolence, intelligence, and fidelity.

Lao-tzu (lou'dzŭ') A Chinese philosopher who lived 604-531 B.C. (approximate dates).

li (lē) In Chinese philosophy this term denotes propriety, which is thought of as the outward expression of inner harmony with the ethical principles of the universe.

Mencius (mĕn'shĭ·ŭs) or **Meng-tse** (mĕng'tsĕ') A Chinese sage who lived 372-288 B.C. (approximate dates).

Taoism (dou'ĭz'm) A religion and philosophy founded by Lao-tzu. It emphasizes conformity to cosmic order and simplicity of social and political organization.

* Many of the words used in this book are peculiar to the particular faiths or religions discussed. For this reason they may not be familiar to the average reader. Because these words are basic to an adequate understanding of these faiths, brief definitions have been provided at the outset of each discussion.

6

Confucianism and Taoism
Religion of Good Ethics

ONE thing that the Communist regime will never be able to do is to get Confucius out of China. Some say it has not tried. Others contend there is no use trying. China's nearly 600,000,000 people know Confucius fully as well as America's millions know the Christ. We do not have a state religion, but we are predominantly Christian. China does not have a state religion, but it is predominantly Confucian.

➤ In China there are approximately fifty million Moslems, around four million Catholics, and approximately one million Protestants. There are untold numbers of Buddhists and members of most of the major religions of the world. But it is Confucianism and Taoism that dominate the religious scene, and it is Confucius whom Chinese love, honor, and obey when it comes to philosophy and teaching for the inner life. He is as indigenous as the rice fields and as much of a legend and reality as China's ancient wall.

But the famous and venerable Confucius—the tall, slender sage of the ages with the reddish beard and the jolly twinkle in his eyes—is quite a match for the Communists, and it is safe to say he will outlive them all. Perhaps there is nothing unusual in this, for prophets always have outlived secular rulers. But the wise and witty Confucius never wanted to be a prophet in the first place.

He was an idealist, a teacher, and a philosopher. He was also a very practical man. Looking out upon the world, he found it preposterous that there should be so much suffering when it could be cured through brotherhood and feelings of good will. He felt that it was unnecessary that there should be so much crime when it is inherent in man's nature to be good. He also loathed the fact that there was so much injustice when we know we must all live together and must all die one day and leave the earth to our offspring.

Confucius had an idea that he could do something about improving the world. He figured that if each generation could be persuaded to benefit by the mistakes and achievements of the past, civilization would make immeasurable strides toward a better future. But to do that, it was necessary for individuals to live the good life, and it was even more necessary for rulers to live effectively.

Now, what can any regime say about that? Where is the government who will oppose such a point of view without incriminating itself? Not even the Communists can argue against that. It is like being against sin. There are simply no two ways about it. That was the secret of the greatness of Confucius. The things he said, the axioms, aphorisms, and attitudes he expressed, represented slumbering giants of truth in the heart of every man.

TRUTH BOTH ANCIENT AND MODERN

Although Confucius lived 2,500 years ago, his teachings are startlingly contemporary. Where he spoke to the people, the ancient ox carts rumbled by. Where he sat with his pupils, primitive torches shed their light over his "classroom." And those who copied down his sayings made their copies by writing laboriously on papyrus sheets. Yet what he *said* still sounds like truth that should be repeated on any television program today.

Confucius said, "Government consists of the correct choice of officials. One must elevate the just men, so that they can exert pressure upon the crooked men, for in this way the crooked may be made straight."

Once when he was asked what made him most sad about the world, he said, "The fact that virtue is not cultivated, that knowledge is not made clear, that people hear of duty and do not practice it, that those who know they are evil do nothing to improve themselves. These are the things that make me sad."

Although Confucius lived in the days of feudalism, five hundred years before Jesus, he sounds as if he already suspected the coming of the Christian faith so far as its ethics are concerned. But he never wanted to start a religion.

"You speak of serving gods," he once remarked to his followers, "but how shall you serve gods when you have not yet learned how to serve men?"

They asked him about life after death, and he replied, "We do not yet know about the present life; how can we know about death?"

They wanted a definition of a gentleman, and he told them, "A gentleman is one who is troubled by his shortcomings."

He said he had been summoned to be a transmitter of truth. That was what he believed himself to be. He had no intention of setting himself up as one whom the gods had fashioned. Being a Shankara, a Buddha, a Zoroaster, or a Moses was far from his mind.

Confucius was born unheralded in the province of Lu in the district of Ch'ang P'ing in the city of Chow in 551 B.C.

His father was a seventy-year-old soldier, and the family name was K'ung. His mother was Ching-Tsai, and he was named Ch'iu K'ung. The principal thing that set him apart from other youth was his lust for learning and a precociousness that showed up in music, poetry, and philosophy at an early age. The only characteristic that marked him as unusual was that he believed that man is inherently good, that goodness always outweighs and conquers evil, and that propriety is a cardinal virtue. Another quality that was exceptional was his insistence that a man must practice what he proclaims or else his proclamations are in vain. Therefore, he tried especially hard to live the good life.

Beyond this he was quite an ordinary man. It is even said —though there is some question about it—that he married at nineteen and was the father of a son. He served the province of Lu in various capacities and, following the death of his mother, went into mourning for three years, as was the custom. He must have been an exceptionally sensitive person, for it is said he captured the moods of the people who came to him for advice and had great respect—as wise men do— for what went on in the other person's mind.

Were he living today, he would no doubt have a syndicated column captioned, "Confucius Says . . . ."

A minister friend, who has a reputation for personalizing religion and who has written books on the subject, claims he has gotten many sound ethical ideas from the Sage of Lu. He says that Confucius was the first to tell a man that the more he meditates upon good thoughts, the better will be his world and the world at large. This, my friend contends, is as modern and as psychologically sound as the power of positive thinking!

Confucius never wished to start a religion. He lived during the days of wandering teachers and itinerant philosophers, and he was one of them. No doubt he was the best of them. They called him K'ung the Master or K'ung-fu-tze, a name that was later Latinized by Jesuits into "Confucius." Even in those days it seems to have been commonplace to ask, "What does Confucius say?"

A school grew up around Confucius which at its peak numbered approximately three thousand students. He taught these persons philosophy and music and placed great emphasis upon ethics. His major course might well have been titled "Wisdom to Live By." Since his students insisted on reading religion into his teachings, they said it was a religion of moral order. By this they were referring to moral order in man, in society, and in the world. Confucius had a word for it. He called it *li*.

Other Chinese philosophers also talked of *li*, but none apparently lived *li* or made it as convincing as Confucius. For it must always be remembered that the Confucian ideal of the superior man was put to the test and lived by Confucius himself. *Li* meant not only moral order; it also meant rightness, virtue, and faith and, most of all, propriety. Confucius said, "True manhood consists in realizing your true self and in restoring *li*. Whosoever will realize his true self and restore *li*, the world will follow him."

Confucius strove to do this, and for a time it looked as though the world would follow him. The ruler of the province of Lu invited him to become a member of his cabinet, and in a surprisingly short time a great change took place in the moral order of the land. People lived better and were happier; crime decreased and *li* was honored as the highest good. It did not last because the ruler himself fell from grace, but Confucius said, "Let there be but the right men and the government will flourish; but without these, government decays and ceases."

CONFUCIANISM AND GOD

Because Confucius did not have the benefit of the teaching
and philosophy of Jesus, he evidently did not know that man
needs help beyond himself. He did not seem to know that
man needs God and that without the Fatherhood of God it is
quite impossible to realize the brotherhood of man. His was
a religion of good ethics, but he never seemed to deepen
ethics by fellowship with the divine.

Also he never seemed to comprehend the help of God even
in his own dilemmas. "There are three things," he said,
"which I do not seem able to achieve in the way of a gentleman: virtue which is free from uncertainty; wisdom which is
free from doubts; courage which is free from fear."

Confucius always came back to *li*. *Li* was the stabilizing
force, the technique by which a man is disciplined, the confidence by which a man is sustained. Whatever there is of
spiritual emphasis in his teaching is centered in *li*. He united
li with a central harmony that he described as "the har-
monization of our moral being with the universe."

Whereas Christianity begins with faith in God through
Christ and leads into the knowledge of the brotherhood of
man, and whereas Christianity has to do with the will of
God and the love of Christ, Confucianism begins with man
as a moral being and then leads into a cosmic consciousness
and the hint of God. In Confucianism there are no Savior, no
salvation, and no sacrifice as the Christian understands these
things.

But Confucius did not have religion in mind. Only his
followers did. Did he not say that life consists of manners,
morals, and motives? And did he not emphasize that in their
highest form these qualities are gifts of the spirit which are
inherent in man and which were placed there by the Creator

ready for use? "Virtue," he insisted, "is man's greatest good, and order is heaven's only law."

And what do the Communist leaders think of all this when they look out across the teeming millions and see the devotees of this great sage stream into temples where the tablets of Confucius are displayed and where incense burns in memory of him who is called by his followers "the Superior Man"? What can they say when, at the Altar of Heaven in Peking, the faithful still repeat in their hearts the things Confucius said?

TAOISM

A contemporary of Confucius, Lao-tzu, whose name means "Old Philosopher," probed deeper into the relationship between ethics and religion and between man's qualities and Creative Force. For Lao-tzu this Creative Force was Tao. Tao was the "Way." Tao included whatever mystery and magic binds man to universal law. Confucius was a moralist and Lao-tzu was a mystic. It is said they never met. Some say Lao-tzu never even lived, but others who love Lao-tzu a great deal say that Confucius sat at his feet. Whatever may be true, *li* and Tao were merged by these two men.

Confucius taught people how to be in the world and of the world in order to improve the world. Lao-tzu instructed men how to escape the world and yet how to remake it by following Tao, the Way of the cosmos, the Way of reason, the Way of life, and the Way of evolution. Lao-tzu once said that following the Way did not require the wisdom Confucius advocated nor the brilliance of thought of which he was the master. Lao-tzu said, "Get rid of the wise men, put out the professors, then the people will profit a hundredfold more."

Nonetheless, he agreed with Confucius on morals and the good life, and the two sages also agreed on the ancient Chinese belief in ancestor worship. They could hardly do otherwise, for reverence for the dead had a long and respected tradition among the people. Confucius said, "When parents are alive, they should be served according to the rules of propriety. When they are dead, they should be buried according to the rules of propriety. After they are buried, they should be sacrificed to according to the rules of propriety."

Confucius believed that ancestor worship kept the wisdom and instruction of the ancients ever alive and present among the living. He worshiped tradition and the ancients—if he worshiped anything—and the tombs of the dead were stepping stones to the understanding of heaven.

Is it any wonder, therefore, that when Confucius died at seventy-three, and when Lao-tzu died at an age unknown, the faithful should begin to worship at their graves? Those who loved these teachers wanted to keep alive the wisdom and instruction that the reverend sages had brought. No greater truth had been revealed up to that time, and no men had come nearer to the heart of China or the souls of its people than Master K'ung and the Old Philosopher. Confucianism and Taoism became religions, and their founders became prophets in spite of themselves.

THE TAO TE CHING AND THE ANALECTS

The followers of Confucius and Lao-tzu collected their sayings and philosophies and put them into books that were to become the Bibles of these faiths. The *Tao Te Ching* (*The Book of the Way and of Virtue*) contains the essence of Taoism. Gently and persuasively it tells its readers that heaven arms with love those it would not see destroyed. Im-

ploringly it suggests how the secret of Tao, or the Way, can
best be discovered:

> "Always without desire we must be found,
> If its deepest mystery we would sound;
> But if desire always within us be,
> Its outer fringe is all that we shall see."

As if anticipating the Christian Gospels, which bring us the
wonderful thinking of Jesus Christ, the *Tao Te Ching* says,
"Repay evil with good," and "Walk in the Way and you shall
find peace."

Some scholars say that Confucius wrote nothing, while
others credit him with at least five classics. All critics agree
that the Bible of Confucianism is the *Analects,* which consists
of twenty short chapters penned by his students during his
life and after his death. Reverently and with affection they
recorded their teacher's words: "The Master said, 'He that
is really good can never be unhappy. He that is really wise
can never be perplexed. He that is really brave is never
afraid.' The Master said, 'Behave when away from home as
though you were in the presence of an important guest. Deal
with the common people as if you were officiating at an important sacrifice.' The Master said, 'He who will not worry
about what is far off will soon find something worse than
worry close at hand.' "

Although Confucius was striving to promote an ethical and
social order, as the years passed, those who loved him deepened the implication of his teachings. They held that true
ethics can be attained only if man lives in harmony with
the divine order of the universe. His most famous interpreter
was Mencius, who was born a hundred years after Master
K'ung had died. Mencius was to Confucius what Paul was to
Jesus Christ. He put the essence of Confucianism into "Five

Constant Virtues": propriety, benevolence, righteousness, wisdom, and sincerity.

Mencius summed up the teaching of his master in these treasured words. "To dwell in the wide house of the world, to fill his correct place in the world, to walk in the great Tao of the world . . . , to practice his principles for the good of the people . . . , to be above the power of riches and honor . . . , such is the man who may be called truly great and courageous."

All this is what Confucius said and what Confucius sought to live 2,500 long years ago. Surely he was among the most modern of the ancients and the most contemporary of primitive prophets. Throughout his vast and sprawling country— which is largest and greatest, population-wise, in all the world —his words and thoughts are the people's richest heritage. The Communist leaders well know just what Confucius said, and there are those who say that Karl Marx and Confucius have made a compact to win the day. Did not each emphasize the fact that man must depend upon himself to live the good life, to achieve maturity, and to build a better society and a better world?

If Confucianism is a religion, it is a religion of good ethics without the Christian secret of how the deepest ethics can be attained. What Master K'ung so devoutly believed in, Jesus Christ demonstrated. With all his vaunted wisdom, Confucius never found the formula that the lowly Galilean brought so convincingly and graphically when he said, "But seek ye first the kingdom of God, and his righteousness; and all these things shall be added unto you" (Matthew 6:33, King James Version).

Master K'ung was born great and venerable and wise, but he was born too soon. We wish he might have known the Christ.

Glossary

CHAPTER 7: SHINTO TERMS *

Amaterasu O-Mi-Kami (ā'mä·tä·rä'sōō ō'mē·kä'mē) The principal deity of Shinto. According to mythology, she charged her grandson to descend to the Japanese islands and rule over them. By means of hereditary succession her descendants would continue to rule forever.

Izanagi (ē·zän'ä·gī) One of the deities elected to give birth to the islands of Japan.

Kami (kä'mē) The Shinto term for "gods."

Kojiki (kō'jĭ·kĭ) The oldest extant history of Japan. Together with the Nihongi it comprises the basic text of Shinto tradition.

Mikado (mĭ·kä'dō) A popular title used by foreigners to designate the Emperor of Japan.

Nihongi (nyē'hŏng·gī) The first of six officially compiled annals of Japan.

Shinto (shĭn'tō) The ancient native religion of Japan. As practiced today, it is more an expression of patriotism and promotes the preservation of traditions through its rites connected with public occasions, through sacred pilgrimages, and popular festivals.

torii (tō'rē·ē) A gateway serving as the approach to a Shinto temple. The torii is constructed with slender beams put together in a fashion similar to that of a post and lintel. These beams are often designed with delicately curved lines.

---

* Many of the words used in this book are peculiar to the particular faiths or religions discussed. For this reason they may not be familiar to the average reader. Because these words are basic to an adequate understanding of these faiths, brief definitions have been provided at the outset of each discussion.

84

7

Shinto
Religion of the Way of the Gods

THE religion called Shinto bears the unmistakable mark:
"Made in Japan." Like many other creative productions
of a creative people, it is one of the most unique faiths in all
the world. And like many other products coming out of
Nippon, it is not always fully appreciated by its makers.

Unlike Christianity, Shinto has no founder, no prophet,
no Savior, no creed, no scripture, no theology. Like Christianity it has its churches, schools, and priests, its groups
within groups, and its sects and subsects. It also has approximately thirty million followers and around 100,000 shrines.
Like Hinduism it has been described as a religion based on
belief in many gods or no gods; and like most religions it runs
the gamut from orthodoxy to modernism, from self-denial
to self-aggrandizement, from science to magic, from faith
to fireworks.

Most Japanese are nominally Shintoists in the same sense
that most Americans are nominally Christian. Many Shintoists worship at their own shrines and at Buddhist shrines
and even pick up what they feel is good and profitable in the
Christian faith, to say nothing of also following Confucius.

A Japanese friend of mine put it this way, "Shinto has

withstood bombings, earthquakes, and even the loss of the
emperor's divinity. There is no reason to think it will not
always be with us."

As far as he was concerned, Shinto would not only always
continue to be, but it had always been. To him it was the
most ancient of religions and the most modern. It represented
the faith of a nation, the way of the gods.

KAMI

Shinto's roots lie deep in the fertile soil of mythology. Its
branches are high—as high as Mount Fuji, which lifts its
proud white head to an altitude of 12,425 feet and which itself
is worshiped by many as a goddess.

Shinto is even higher than that. It is as high as the rising
sun, by whose name ninety million people of the islands
identify themselves. The symbol of the rising sun is also im-
printed upon Japan's national flag. The sun is a Shinto goddess with a musical name: Amaterasu O-Mi-Kami—the
Heaven-Shining-Great *Kami*.

Kami is the word to remember. *Kami* tells the Shinto
story. *Kami* is the power that creates, sustains, governs,
and upholds everything in the universe and beyond the universe. *Kami* is God, and *Kami* are the gods. *Kami* is the
élan vital, the life essence, the force, the cause, the effect, the
past, present, and future. Space and time, spacelessness and
timelessness—all is *Kami*. In fact, the Japanese term for the
phrase "way of the gods" is *Kami no michi*. The word "Shinto," which is now commonly and universally known, is said
to have been used by Confucius and made up of *Shen*
(heavenly spirits) and *Tao* (the Way).

If we remember *Kami* and bear in mind that the world
was not created by *Kami* but that the world is *Kami*, it will

help us understand this most interesting faith. For, actually, the Shintoist sees no distinction between created things and creator, between man and god, between material and spiritual qualities. All are one and the same, and the eternal stream of divine consciousness flows in and through all. Differences in divinity may exist, but they are differences of degree and not of kind. Even evil is not evil to the true Shintoist. It is an illusion. Only a person's limited viewpoint makes him look upon evil as something apart from *Kami*. When the Shinto myths speak of demons, they are speaking of disguised *Kami* in forms who serve a purpose and who present a lesson. In short, the Shintoist would agree in part with our modern Christian Scientist who says, "There is no life, truth, intelligence, nor substance in matter. All is infinite Mind and its infinite manifestation, for God is All-in-all. Spirit is immortal Truth. . . ." [1]

When we visit Japan, we see gateways called torii which consist of crosspieces on two uprights. Many of these have beautifully curved lines and delicate carvings, and they tell us when we are approaching a temple or shrine. The torii is a symbol for what the Shintoist thinks of as a floating bridge connecting earth and heaven. It is the rainbow. It is the perch on which the roosters herald the morning whenever the sun goddess, Amaterasu O-Mi-Kami, brings a new day to her beloved people.

In the humblest domestic shrines, on the so-called "god shelves" in Shinto homes, the torii stands, reminding the worshiper of *Kami*. Here, too, stands the sacred mirror, calling to mind the words of the sun goddess who said, "Look upon this mirror as my actual presence." Reflected glory, the shining beauty of the gods, the inner beauty of the human

[1] Mary Baker Eddy, *Science and Health With Key to the Scriptures* (Boston: Trustees Under the Will of Mary Baker G. Eddy, 1934), page 468.

heart, the undisclosed mystery of the human soul—all this is *Kami*.

The true Shintoist lives in a pool of divinity. He is absorbed by it, surrounded by it, lost in it. God is everywhere, and everywhere is God. God is everything, and everything is God. God is in the Shintoist, and he is in God. This does not keep him from being a practical and a realistic person; instead, it makes him practical and realistic. But practicality reminds him that the essence of life is the divine ingredient. And realism causes him always to see everything in the light of its divine spirit. Even the trees—particularly the *sakaki*, which surround the shrines—assure him of the "tree of life." In olden times no tree was ever cut down without a prayer, for the tree symbolizes vitality and fellowship with God.

EMPEROR WORSHIP

When my friend said that Shinto had outlived the loss of the emperor's divinity, he was, of course, referring to one of the most revolutionary acts that ever happened to a nation's religious life anywhere: The emperor was forced to give up his spiritual title in 1946. To understand and appreciate the once vaunted divinity of Japanese emperors, we must open the histories of old Japan, books called the *Kojiki* and *Nihongi*. In these chronicles written in the eighth century A.D. we learn that Japan itself was born in heaven at the time of creation. It was planned by a trinity of *Kami* who said, in effect, "Let us make the earth and include a special paradise."

A god and a goddess, Izanagi and Izanami, are often referred to as the Shinto Adam and Eve and are considered as being the first persons who were both mortal and immortal. The Shintoists believe that these deities stood on the floating bridge of heaven and gazed down upon the aimless, drifting land. Then with a jeweled spear Izanagi stirred up a portion of the formless earth. When he had fashioned an island, he drew out the spear, and the beauty dripping from the jewel created some very special islands that are now Japan.

The spiritual head of this paradise obviously had to be a spiritually personalized being. He came as the offspring of the sun goddess Amaterasu O-Mi-Kami, and the people who descended from Izanagi and Izanami became his subjects—divine in themselves. Beside him on his throne was the sacred mirror. The sovereign and the sun goddess became a representation of the unity of heaven and earth in what the Shintoist believes is the holiest and loveliest land in all the world. Incidentally, even Marco Polo, who visited the islands six hundred years ago and who referred to the inhabitants as heathen and cannibals, reported:

"The sea in which Zipangu [Japan] is situated is called the Sea of Chin [China]. . . . It is said that of the trees which grow in [the islands], there are none that do not yield a fragrant smell. . . .

"It is impossible to estimate the value of the gold and other articles . . . ." [2]

So the deification of the emperor was carried to a height in Shintoism far beyond that found in any other religious culture. Some have compared it to the Jewish adoration of Jehovah. Others have said it far surpassed the Roman Catholic's affection for the pope. It was here, at this most sacred and sensitive spot, that the defeat of Japan brought a great blow to the Shintoists on January 1, 1946. At that time Emperor Hirohito denied that he was divine.

By the adoption of the postwar constitution in 1947 the

[2] *The Travels of Marco Polo*, revised from Marsden's translation and edited by Manuel Komroff (New York: Random House; copyright by Boni and Liveright), Book III, chapter 4.

Japanese people not only renounced forever the right to wage war or maintain military forces of any kind, but they also stripped the emperor of all pretensions of divinity. Henceforth he was to be just another secular ruler deriving his authority not from the Heaven-Shining-Great *Kami* but from the supreme will of the people. The justification on the part of the victors was, of course, not to destroy a peoples' faith but to prevent the continuation of a state-supported religious propaganda system and the favoritism and fanaticism that had been the outgrowth of emperor worship.

The impact of this tradition-breaking act was so tremendous that many Japanese could not fully comprehend it. It happened on paper but not in their hearts. Though the emperor publicly renounced his right to divinity, his act was construed as one in which he had no choice. It was the result of surrender and defeat on the part of the Japanese military powers. To the traditional Shintoist the emperor of the Land of the Rising Sun would ever continue to be a symbol of heaven as well as a symbol of the state.

There were, however, cold facts to be considered. If the emperor was truly in the succession of the sons of heaven, why did he not save himself by some heavenly miracle? Why could he not call down the hosts of *Kami* and prove his sacred heritage? Now the state Shinto was abolished. Patriotism and religion no longer walked hand in hand. Could there still be compunction on the part of the people to feel that one who was both god and man had dwelt in their midst, lived in the inviolable sanctuary of the sacred palace, and bore in his person the imprint of a holiness beyond that of the common man? State Shinto, which was born in glory, died in disillusionment and despair as an institutionalized form. But its spirit still lives along with sectarian Shinto, and it lives strongly.

The Threat of Buddhism

My friend was right. Shinto withstood the loss of its vicar of heaven. He might also have added that it withstood the impact of Buddhism. For many years the religion of Gautama, the Buddha has threatened Shinto from without and within. The struggle began in A.D. 552 when a king of Korea, seeking to form an alliance with Japan, sent a huge golden statue of the Buddha to the emperor as a gift. With it came Buddhist priests and teachers.

According to the story the statue was enshrined in the home of the chief minister despite violent Shinto opposition. Suddenly an epidemic of smallpox broke out, and it was taken as a sign that the *Kami* were highly displeased that the Buddha had been so honored. The emperor quickly ordered the statue thrown into a canal. Shortly thereafter the gods of Buddhism were apparently aroused, because lightning struck the imperial palace. So Buddha's statue was reverently fished out of the canal and given a proper place in a newly built temple.

With Buddhism came Chinese writing and Chinese culture and even Chinese language. This caused the Japanese to take a new look at themselves, and, eventually, they took a new interest in their religion—a religion that, until the Buddha came, had been without a name. The religion of the *Kami* now came to be called Shinto.

One thing that prevented Shinto's being destroyed by its encounter with Buddhism was its mythology. Within the myths were hidden secrets transmitted (until the eighth century) by oral tradition. All primitive religions had their myths with meanings, but few, if any, had the detailed and explicit elements inherent in the *Kojiki* and *Nihongi* records. The narratives cannot be understood unless the reader is

willing to give the writings—lewd and extravagant though
they may be—the benefit of a sacramental sanction.

Preliterate Japanese found the greatest wonder and phenomenon of all in life—particularly in sex and birth. Their
deities are endowed with exaggerated and vivid imaginations
and are players in dramas that often seem vulgar and bizarre.
But always there are hidden meanings, and always these
stories return to the true essence: the reality of the unseen.
For the untutored Shintoist the symbolism may not go deep,
but for the enlightened follower the moral within the myth
is clearly discernible. And this, of course, is true in every
religion. God—whether in the Christian sense or, as *Kami*,
in Shinto—means different things to different people for the
simple reason that people are different.

This is also why Shinto shrines and Shinto god shelves
are elaborate or simple depending upon the bent of mind
of the worshiper. The shrine is actually a chapel surrounded
by a sacred fence and entered through a gate. The worshiper
proceeds to the outer shrine. There he pauses to purify
his hands and mouth with holy water, which is in a small
trough. Then, approaching nearer, he claps his hands. He
does this not to announce to the gods that he has come but
rather as an act of reverent joy and a gesture of praise. He
bows low, rings the bell or strikes the gong, then kneels with
head to the floor and devotes himself to thoughtful worship.

Purity and reverence are the two greatest qualities in
Shinto, and, because of this fact, these are also the outstand-
ing characteristics of the Japanese people. Prayers of suppli-
cation as we know them are unknown in Shinto.

The Shintoist does not seek answers to the riddles of suffering and pain as do Christians and many persons who hold
other beliefs. His devotion is a spiritual interlude whose aim
is to deepen the purity of his life and encourage more rever-

ence in his thoughts. He sees himself as part of the *Kami* consciousness, created to find joy in life and believing himself worthy and capable of experiencing it. Perhaps he does not fully appreciate the meaning of all this, but it is an accepted part of his natural spiritual heritage.

There is little concern about life after death and even less about salvation in Shinto. It has no eschatology. There are no cemeteries around Shinto shrines. Death is something still to be overcome. Death is actually an illusion and does not exist in a spiritual sense, and the Shintoist seeks not to countenance it. "To get religion like a Christian," said a Japanese student, "to study it like a Buddhist, to live it like a Confucianist, and to enjoy it like the Shintoist, this is a good arrangement." He meant that the way of the gods is always good and that since Shinto makes no distinction between what is secular and what is spiritual, it is unnecessary to have rules, regulations, or commandments.

Because the gods made man, he instinctively knows what is good. How or why should the gods have made him otherwise? Dogmas about original sin or man's depravity would be unthinkable to the Shintoist. Life is good, the gods are noble, Japan is heavenly, and what more should a person demand of religion than this intuitive awareness and a deepened call to purity and reverence? And that is why, when the Shintoist has finished his devotion, he bows in grateful worship, leaves a contribution in the money box, bows again, and leaves refreshed. He then goes on his way where the torii reminds him of the bridge between heaven and earth.

Shinto priests have no sermons to preach. They do not speak of any eternal punishment, purgatory, or hell from which people must be saved, nor do they teach about any heaven for which there must be theological preparation. Even ancestors are not worshiped in Shinto; they are merely re-

spected and remembered with special devotions. The priests
are examples for the people in much the same sense that lay
ministers are considered models of behavior in such groups as
the Mennonites and many others. Often they have secular
jobs that support them. They take care of the sacred objects
in the shrines, especially in the inner shrine, where the *shintai*
—the god body or relic—is enshrined. The *shintai* may be
a mirror or a stone or a fetish of some type which is touched
only by the priests and only during festival periods.

THE PURIFICATION FESTIVAL

The purification festival has always been an important
observance in Shinto and throughout Japan, where "cleanli-
ness is next to godliness." In the days of the mikados, who
were considered as being divinely appointed, the people sym-
bolically cleansed their bodies by rubbing bits of paper over
their skin and then burning the papers or throwing them into
a river. The mikado, representing the sun goddess, then pro-
nounced the people clean in body and mind. This custom,
rooted in the belief that individual impurity may have dread-
ful consequences, is still part of the Shinto way of life.

Shintoists claim that theirs is a good way, this way of
the gods. They say that it is a healthy, wholesome religion
and a pure faith in spite of the fact that it is becoming in-
creasingly influenced by Buddhism, Confucianism, and
American Christianity. But the Shinto that is the pure religion of *Kami* consciousness was made in Japan. According to the record, it has never been exported in any appre-
ciable quantity to spiritual seekers elsewhere in the great
world. According to the ancient books, the outside world is
but a replica of the heavenly world of which Japan is most
heavenly of all.

Glossary

CHAPTER 8: ISLAMIC TERMS *

Allah (äl'ä) The Supreme Being of Islam.

caliph (kā'lǐf) A successor of Mohammed; also the title used by spiritual or temporal rulers in Moslem countries.

Fatima (fä'tē·mä) Mohammed's favorite daughter.

Hadith (hà·dēth') A body of traditions which dates back to Mohammed and his companions.

hadj (hăj) A pilgrimage to a holy place, especially to Mecca.

hegira (hē·jī'rà) Mohammed's flight from Mecca, A.D. 622.

imam (ǐ·mäm') A Moslem priest or any person considered as an authority in Islamic theology and law.

Islam (ǐs'läm) Literally, this word means "submission to the will of God." It refers to the religion of Moslems. Their creed is: There is no god but Allah, and Mohammed is his prophet.

Kaaba (kä'bà) A small stone building located in the court of the Great Mosque at Mecca. It contains the famed Black Stone, which is supposed to have been given by Gabriel to Abraham.

Koran (kô·rän') The scriptures of the Moslems, which contain the professed revelations to Mohammed.

Mahdi (mä'dē) This title means "the guided one" and refers to a leader who will fill the earth with righteousness. The Sunnites believe he is yet to appear; the Shiites hold that the last imam, who disappeared about 874, will one day reappear as the Mahdi.

Mecca (měk'à) A city in Arabia which is the birthplace of Mohammed. Moslems consider it holy.

Medina (mà·dē'nä) Holy City of Islam. It is named for Mohammed. It was formerly called Yathrib.

* Many of the words used in this book are peculiar to the particular faiths or religions discussed. For this reason they may not be familiar to the average reader. Because these words are basic to an adequate understanding of these faiths, brief definitions have been provided at the outset of each discussion.

95

Mohammed (mô·hăm'ĕd) Prophet of Islam.

Moslem (mŏz'lĕm) An orthodox follower of Mohammed.

mosque (mŏsk) An Islamic place of public worship.

muezzin (mû·ĕz'ĭn) A Moslem crier who denotes the hour of prayer.

mulla (mŭl'å) A teacher of Islamic laws and doctrines.

Omar (ō'mår) Second Moslem caliph, also principal advisor to the first caliph, Abu Bakr.

purdah (pûr'då) A screen or veil used by Moslem women to ensure them against public observation.

Ramadan (răm'å·dán') The ninth month of the Moslem year, which is a time of strict fasting.

salat (så·lāt') The Moslem daily ritual prayer.

Shiites (shē'īts) A branch of the Moslems. They reject the first three caliphs and insist that Ali, Mohammed's son-in-law, was the first rightful successor to Mohammed.

Sufi (sōō'fê) A Moslem mystic and ascetic.

Sunnites (sōōn'īts) A Moslem sect, the members of which acknowledge the first four caliphs as the rightful successors of Mohammed.

sura (sōō'rå) A chapter of the Koran.

CHAPTER

8

Islam
Religion of the Book

THERE is one thing about Islam I will never forget:
the muezzin call from the minaret. The muezzin, a
Moslem crier, robed in a dark gown and wearing a flowing
turban, climbs the slender, lofty tower called the minaret.
Here, on a platform encircled by a balustrade, he stands like
a watcher against the sky. Then he cups his hands over his
lips and calls loudly, in Arabic, "There is no God but Allah!
Mohammed is the messenger of Allah! Come to prayer, come
to prayer!"

I am afraid that this type of muezzin call will soon be a
thing of the past, for modern inventions are catching up with
this ancient custom. In many mosques loud-speakers have
been installed or the call has been entirely abandoned. But
in some devout Moslem cities in the Middle East you can
still hear it, particularly on Friday, which is the Islam Sabbath.

In the early days of this rugged faith, the followers of
Mohammed paused in their work and faced the Holy City
of Mecca in Hejaz, Arabia. With the palms of their hands
pressed together, they stood for a moment, then knelt, touch-
ing their foreheads to the ground. The nearly 430,000,000

people of Islam are still enjoined to do this, but many of the
imams, or Moslem ministers, will tell you, "The world is
creeping in and our religion is changing."

EMPHASIS ON PRAYER

Islam was always a praying faith. One of its members, a
young man with a good Moslem name, Abdullah Igram, said
to me, "My earliest recollection is a prayer that begins,
'In the name of God, the Merciful, the Beneficent.' I learned
this literally at my mother's knee. I heard my father use it,
and he said that it came from the holy Koran. It was an inspiring prayer, and it is with me today, helping me in the
important moments of my life."
Then he recited the prayer:

"In the name of Allah, the Merciful, the Beneficent,
  Praise be to Allah, Lord of the worlds,
  The Beneficent, the Merciful,
  Master of the day of Requital.
  Thee do we serve and thee do we beseech for help;
  Guide us on the right path,
  The path of those upon whom thou hast bestowed favors,
  Not those upon whom wrath is brought down,
  Nor those who go astray."

You will find this prayer at the very beginning of the
sacred scripture of Islam, the Koran. It is the Koran that
unites the people and shapes their world; it is the Koran that
Moslems learn literally at their mother's knee. Though the
muezzin call should be silenced, though prayer practices
should wane, the people of Islam vow that the Koran will
never be neglected or defamed. Islam is the religion of this
book.

THE KORAN

Moslems believe that the Koran or *Quran* is the true and
inspired word of God transmitted to the prophet Mohammed
by the angel Gabriel. They will tell you that among the many
holy writings of the world it alone has never been revised
or changed. It has 114 suras or chapters, and the Moslems
believe that its 77,639 words are all holy. Its instructions and
guidance for living the good life and obtaining salvation are
inviolable. The Koran is undefiled, unmatched, and uncreated, they say. It existed in heaven since the beginning
of time and awaited the coming of the one who was most
worthy to receive it—Mohammed, the prophet of Allah.

Mohammed was born 570 years after the birth of Christ.
As a boy he lived in Mecca and his name was Ubu'l Kassim.
Because his father died when Ubu'l was two months old, he
lived first with his grandfather and then with an uncle, Abu
Talib, who often took him on caravan journeys to distant
trading posts. Mecca was the crossroads of the world, the
thoroughfare between India and Persia, Syria, and Greece.
It was a place where travelers rested and merchants managed
their affairs. It was also a city where priests and minor
prophets of strange religions sought to serve the travelers'
spiritual needs.

Religion was big business in Mecca. Located here were
temples and shrines to many nature gods, and the city also
boasted of the famous Black Stone, which was oval in shape
and slightly larger than a pomegranate and which was said
to work miracles. Legends insisted that the stone was once
pure white but that it turned black because it grieved over
the sins of men. A cubelike building called the Kaaba housed
the sacred stone, and a number of images—360 of them—
stood around it and were tended by priests who collected ex-

travagant fees from persons who came for worship and
prayers.

A small group of Meccans called "the Hunafa" (seekers)
were disturbed at this commercialization of religion and
Ubu'l Kassim agreed with them. He believed, as did the
Hunafa, that the stone was actually one that the angel
Gabriel gave to Abraham long ago. He also believed that
the Kaaba itself had been built in heaven and that Abraham
and his son Ishmael built this one in Mecca directly under
the heavenly spot where the eternal Kaaba stands. And, like
most devout Hunafa, Ubu'l Kassim believed the prophecy
that one day a prophet would appear and re-establish the
Kaaba as the true God's earthly home.

ALLAH'S MESSENGER

As a young man Ubu'l Kassim often accompanied his
uncle on caravan journeys to Palestine. Here he met Jews
who worshiped one God, Yahweh, and Christians who, so he
thought, worshiped three gods—Father, Son, and Holy Spirit.
He also met Hindus who claimed there were many representations of the one God, Brahma, and he met people of Asia
who worshiped gods of the wind and sun and rain.

It seemed to Ubu'l Kassim that all people had one thing
in common: Everyone was searching for God. And Ubu'l
was searching. Whenever he returned to the Kaaba and
walked among the 360 statues, he asked himself, "Are there
many gods in the universe, or is there one? Who is the true
God? How can I know him, and what does he want me to
do with my life?"

People said Ubu'l Kassim was a very lucky man. He had
grown successful in business, and his wife was very rich, but
still he was sad and serious and continually made lonely pil-

grimages to a cave on Mount Hira. The people did not know
about his quest, nor did they know that one night a great light
filled the cave where he prayed. Then in the course of the
experience a voice said to him, "Read!"

Ubu'l Kassim replied, "I cannot read. I have never learned
to read."

A second and a third time the voice ordered, "Read!"

"What shall I read?" Ubu'l asked.

Then, in a vision, words appeared to him; and the voice
said, "Read: In the name of Allah who created, who created
man from a clot. Read: And thy lord is most bounteous who
teacheth by the pen, teacheth man that which he knew not.
Verily, man is rebellious. He thinketh himself independent.
Lo, unto thy lord is the return!"

When Ubu'l Kassim awoke from the trance, day was dawn-
ing. Beyond him lay the city of Mecca with its Kaaba and
its many gods and its sacred stone. As he looked toward the
scene, he heard the heavenly voice saying, "O Mohammed!
Thou art Allah's messenger!"

"Who are you?" he cried. "Let me see your face!"

"I am Gabriel," said the voice. And Ubu'l Kassim saw
the angel standing against the sky, holding a silken shawl
covered with the words he had earlier been asked to read.
No matter which way he turned, the angel Gabriel was
always before his eyes, saying to him, "You are no longer
Ubu'l Kassim. You are Mohammed, the prophet of Allah!"
Then the voice was stilled and the vision ended.

THE TEACHINGS OF THE BOOK

This is how Islam was born. It was born with a vision,
and it is the flaming story of Mohammed, prophet of Allah,
and his victory over the 360 false gods and false prophets in

the city of Mecca. It is the account of the unification of the
divided and dispersed Arab people. It is the story of plot
and counterplot against the Prophet's life, of miracles of
escape from oppressors and miracles of protection from infidel mobs. It is the drama of the hegira, the Prophet's flight
from Mecca to Yathrib, which occurred in A.D. 622 and which
serves as the beginning of the Moslem era. It is the historic
record of Mohammed's life in Medina, where he converted
people to the faith, and of his return to Mecca and the capture of the city in Allah's holy name.

It is the tender narrative of a prophet who knelt before
the sacred stone, who returned the Kaaba to the true God,
and who called his city holy. It is the saga of Islam, which
means "submission to the will of God," and of the Moslem
faith, which means surrender to God. But most of all it is
the story of a book, the holy Koran, which means "the
reading."

Where did the book come from if not from God? How
could an illiterate man write a profoundly philosophical and
prophetic book that traces the plan of salvation from Moses
through Jesus and onward to Mohammed? How could
Ubu'l Kassim have put into writing the wondrous ideas that
comprise the most noble, poetic, and impressive Arabic classic
in all the world unless God wrote through him as his instru-
ment? Listen to the beauty of the prayer entitled "The
Morning Hours" and then ask yourself what a Moslem
asked me: "Could an uneducated camel driver have written
these words?"

"By the morning hours,
And by the night when it is stillest,
Thy Lord hath not forsaken thee nor doth he hate thee;
Verily, the latter portion will be better for thee
Than was the former,

Verily thy Lord will give unto thee so that thou wilt surely be
content.
Did he not find thee an orphan and protect thee?
Did he not find thee wandering and direct thee?
Did he not find thee destitute and enrich thee?
Therefore the orphan oppress not,
Therefore the beggar drive not away,
Therefore of the bounty of thy Lord be thy discourse."

When the Prophet died in A.D. 632 at the age of sixty-two,
it was the Koran that took his place among the affections of
his people. At early dawn on the day of his death he went
into the mosque to pray. He said it was his farewell pilgrimage. People said, "He cannot die! He is the prophet of Allah!"
Then, later in the day, when the rumor spread that he had
passed away, one of his disciples, Omar, assured the people
that it was not true.

But the disciple Abu Bakr went in to where the Prophet
lay, kissed the dead man's forehead, and came to address the
people. Above the loud protest of Omar, Abu Bakr cried
out, "O people! As for you who used to worship Mohammed,
Mohammed is dead. But as for you who used to worship
Allah, Allah is alive and dieth not! Does not the holy Koran
say, 'Mohammed is but a messenger, messengers the like of
whom have passed away before him'? Will it be that, when
he dieth or is slain, ye will turn back on your heels? He who
turneth back doth not hurt Allah, and Allah will reward the
thankful."

And Omar said, "When I heard Abu Bakr recite that
verse from the holy Koran, my feet were cut from beneath
me and I fell to the ground, for I knew that Allah's messenger
was dead. May Allah bless and keep him!"

Mohammed was dead, but his passing endowed the Koran
with ever greater life. It is said that when a Moslem recites

from these sacred writings, the devil cannot harm him.
When the wisest of Arabs think they are wise, they need but
read this book to be humbled. When a follower of Islam goes
to the mosque, the words of the Koran are on his mind and
in his heart. Because they love the Koran so much, many a
devout Moslem has memorized it in its entirety.

Once in Beirut, India, there was a shipwreck not far from
the harbor. The report spread through the city that help was
needed. I ran toward the scene of the mishap and, in trying
to take a short cut, lost my way. Breathlessly I paused to
ask directions of a Moslem who sat in his doorway reciting
words from the Koran over a string of beads. As he quietly
gave me the directions, I asked impatiently, "Aren't you coming along? People may be drowning!"

The man shrugged his shoulders and said, "It is the will
of Allah." Then he went back to his beads, which, on the
Moslem rosary, number ninety-nine—each a symbol for one
of the ninety-nine beautiful names for God.

CUSTOMS AND BELIEFS

The beautiful name of Jesus occurs many times in the
Koran, and the fifth sura, entitled "The Table Spread," de-
rives its name from the event of the Passover. Moslems hold
Jesus in high regard, and in Damascus, at one of the world's
greatest mosques, I was shown a minaret called the minaret of
Jesus. My Islamic friend assured me that when Jesus returned to earth again, he would first come to this particular
minaret and give the call to prayer.

I often thought of the Koran and its rules and customs
when I saw Moslem women in purdah—heavily veiled, some
completely covered from head to foot in a tentlike garment.
It has only narrow slits made in the cloth which permit the

woman to see. The Koran does not specifically order such extreme veiling, but the custom may have originated from its instructions concerning the behavior of men who wished to speak to the wives of Mohammed. It says that they should do so only through a curtain. "That," says the holy book, "is purer for your hearts and for their hearts."

Polygamy was permitted among Moslems, and Mohammed's wives, who were ten in number, were considered examples of virtuous living. This was true in spite of the fact that they occasionally showed feelings of jealousy and ill temper.

After Mohammed's death, Abu Bakr, the father of the Prophet's favorite wife, Aisha, was elected caliph, or Moslem leader. As is usually the case, however, other factions and other aspirants to leadership quickly appeared, some with claims to revelations and prophecies.

Such a group were the Shiites, who arose to say that Ali, the husband of Mohammed's favorite daughter, Fatima, was the rightful heir to the Prophet's throne. The larger group, called Sunnites, objected, but the Shiites grew in numbers anyway. This latter group refer to their leaders as imams rather than caliphs. The imam twelfth removed from Ali is called "Mahdi" or "the guided one," and the Shiites claim, that he did not die but has been miraculously preserved and concealed by Allah. They also believe strongly that some day he will appear and conquer the world.

VARIED MOSLEM GROUPS

Many groups, sects, and movements have appeared in the history of Moslemism. Today there are Sufis, who are mystics, and there are Ulamas, who are mullas, or jurists of the faith. There are self-appointed caliphs and self-styled imams.

There are numerous sects within Islam even in the United States. Bearing witness to the large number of Moslems in America is a newly-built, inspiring Islamic Center located in Washington, D. C.

The one truly cohesive force within the far-flung, world-wide boundaries of the Moslem world, however, is the Koran. Like the Kaaba the Koran is believed to be an exact copy of the original, which exists in heaven.

The Koran has been severely judged by critics both inside and outside the faith. Some say it is a plagiarism of Judaeo-Christian writings, mixed with dreamy reveries and fables conjured up by the bold imagination of Ubu'l Kassim. Thomas Carlyle's classic statement about the Koran has been widely quoted. He said that it was as toilsome reading as he ever undertook. He spoke of it as a wearisome, confused jumble. But Islam loves this book, has carried it through a long series of holy wars, has sworn by it, died by it, and may one day even live for it in unity and peace.

MAJOR MOSLEM BELIEFS

The Koran, the *hadith* (Moslem traditions), and the prophet Mohammed are Allah's trinity of faith and order for the people of Islam. They prescribe "Five Pillars of Faith" and "Six Articles of Belief."

The Five Pillars are:

1. The *shahadah,* or recitation, says, "There is no God but Allah; Mohammed is the messenger of Allah."

2. The *salat,* or daily prayer, is spoken in Arabic by devout Moslems five times each twenty-four hours. As they say these prayers, they face toward Mecca.

3. The *zakat* is a tithe, which every Moslem is expected

to donate as his portion toward the expansion of the faith and the support of the poor.

4. Every Moslem is expected to observe Ramadan, which is the ninth month of the Moslem calendar. A strict fast is kept during the daylight hours of Ramadan as a commemoration of the first revelation of the Koran.

5. Every loyal Moslem is expected to make at least one pilgrimage or *hadj* to Mecca during his lifetime. As he enters the Holy City, he dons a seamless gown and, among other ceremonial acts, walks in prayer seven times around the sacred Kaaba.

The Six Articles of Belief, which are particularly important to Moslems, are:

1. God is one, and this one is Allah.
2. The Koran is Allah's truly inspired book.
3. God's angels are God's messengers and aids, and there are evil spirits to oppose them.
4. God sent his prophets to earth at stated times and for stated purposes. The last and greatest of the prophets was Mohammed.
5. The Day of Judgment will find good and evil deeds weighed in the balance, and souls will pass to heaven or hell on a bridge "finer than a hair and sharper than a sword."
6. The lives and acts of men are foreordained by an all-knowing God, but this does not eliminate the exercise of free will.

Besides these main principles there are moral codes, which my Moslem friends have impressed upon me by their practice and demonstration. The Koran speaks against stealing, lying, bearing false witness, becoming intoxicated, eating pork, gambling, and worshiping false gods. It urges them to carry the words and thoughts of Allah continually in their hearts, and exhorts them to be good to the poor, to be modest, peace-loving, generous, and kind.

Islam rightfully claims that no other religion has been so successful in demonstrating equality of race and rank as has the faith of Mohammed. Nowhere in the world, says the Moslem, is worship so open and free as in the mosque. No-where do people meet in a nobler sense of brotherhood and fraternity. Wash yourself scrupulously clean, remove your shoes, cleanse your heart, and enter the domed house of the Lord. They say they should do this often—five times a day. How can persons not obey this when the holy Koran itself says in one of its loveliest sutras: "O you who believe! When the call is made for prayer . . . then hasten to the remembrance of your God! Leave off your trading . . . and when the prayer is ended, then disperse in the land and seek of Allah's bounty, and remember Allah much, that ye may be successful! There is no God but Allah! Mohammed is the messenger of Allah! Come to prayer! Come to prayer!"

Yes, there is one thing about Islam which I will never forget. It is the muezzin call from the minaret.

Glossary

CHAPTER 9: CHRISTIAN TERMS *

Anabaptist (ăn'á·băp'tĭst) One of a group that arose among the followers of Zwingli in 1523 in Zurich, Switzerland.

Bethlehem (bĕth'lĕ-ĕm) A town in Judea which is the birthplace of Jesus.

Calvin (kăl'vĭn), **John.** French Protestant Reformer (1509-64).

Copt (kŏpt) A member of the ancient Christian church of Egypt.

Eastern Orthodox Church A body of believers whose communion was first formed in the ninth century when the separation between the Eastern and Western Catholic churches took place.

Golgotha (gŏl'gô-thá) Calvary, the place of Jesus' Crucifixion.

Groote (ĸrō'tĕ), **Ger'hard** (ĸā'rärt) Dutch religious reformer (1340-84).

Huss (hŭs), **John.** Bohemian religious reformer (1369-1415).

Knox (nŏks), **John.** Scottish reformer and statesman (1505-72).

Logos (lŏg'ŏs) The Word of God.

Moravian (mô-rā'vĭ-ăn) A member of a Protestant Christian sect established in 1467 in Bohemia. They were known first as the Bohemian Brothers.

Savonarola (săv'ô-nà·rō'lá), **Girolamo** jê·rô'lä-mô) Italian reformer (1452-98).

Unitarian (ū'nĭ·târ'ĭ·ăn) One who does not believe in the doctrine of the Trinity.

Via Dolorosa (vī'á dŏl'ô-rō'sá) The traditional route taken by

---

* Many of the words used in this book are peculiar to the particular faiths or religions discussed. For this reason they may not be familiar to the average reader. Because these words are basic to an adequate understanding of these faiths, brief definitions have been provided at the outset of each discussion.

109

Jesus Christ as he made his way from Pilate's judgment hall to Golgotha.

Waldenses (wŏl·dĕn'sēz) A sect of dissenters from the Roman Catholic Church. It was founded by Peter Waldo, a merchant of Lyon in the twelfth century.

Wycliffe (wĭk'lĭf), **John.** English religious reformer and Bible translator (1320?-84).

Zwingli (tsvĭng'lē), **Huldreich** (hō͞ol'drĭĸ) Swiss Reformation leader (1484-1531).

CHAPTER

9

Christianity
Religion of the Revelation of God in Christ

OF ALL religious narratives in the world, none is more
beautiful than that which begins, "Now when Jesus was
born in Bethlehem of Judea . . ." (Matthew 2:1).

Of all spiritual teachings that have been presented through
heaven's holy men, none are more sublime than those that
say, "Blessed are the poor in spirit, for theirs is the kingdom
of heaven" (Matthew 5:3).

Of all the prayers that prophets prayed and of all the
love that they shared, no prayer has ever brought the nature
of God nearer or made it clearer than the prayer that begins, "Our Father who art in heaven . . ." (Matthew 6:9).

Of all the evidences of the power and glory of messiahship
to which the world's scriptures testify, none lives deeper in
the souls of men than the report, "You are the Christ, the
Son of the living God" (Matthew 16:16).

Of all the promises that the scriptures of mankind hold
out to men, of all the gospels of good news and hope with
which the world is filled, no promise rings with greater hope
than the words, "Because I live, you will live also" (John
14:19).

111

FROM BETHLEHEM TO GOLGOTHA

Reliving the Christian story, I stood in the Shepherds' Field near Bethlehem one holy night and imagined—as every pilgrim does—that I heard the angels' song. For Christianity is a sentimental faith—a simple, believing, trusting faith.

In the Church of the Nativity I knelt at the star-marked manger, realizing more than ever that Christianity has not left unsatisfied the universal human desire to worship or the wish to probe the mysteries of the supernatural.

In Nazareth I said to myself, "Perhaps it was here that he worked. Here is where the carpenter shop may have stood." Christianity more than any other faith is conscious of the close relationship of work and worship.

Beside the Sea of Galilee I imagined I heard him say, "Follow me, and I will make you fishers of men" (Matthew 4:19). For the religion of the Christ is a religion of vocation.

In Bethany and Bethphage, where he loved to visit, I walked among the people. Like every other Christian traveler I was escorted down into a tomb some twenty feet within the earth. Perhaps it was here, outside this silent grave, that he stood and called in a loud voice, "Lazarus, come out" (John 11:43). Christianity has always insisted that death does not ultimately have the last word. Death is an enemy to be overcome, a mystery to be solved, a victory to be won.

I went to "dark Gethsemane" where olive trees, reminiscent of his loneliness, stand in the hallowed garden. Nearby, inside a church, I found enshrined the stone on which, it is said, he prayed that night. Like every other man who loves his faith I knelt down, believing that Christianity in a very special way has found and revealed the creative power of prayer.

I walked the Via Dolorosa, the way of sorrow. There are always those who follow this winding path and pray at the stations. There are always those who pause reverently and silently as I did, and, reflective, they remember his example and are ashamed of their uncommitted lives.

And then I went to Golgotha. There are two places called Golgotha in Jerusalem, and you may take your choice or visit both. One, elaborately sanctified, is found inside the present city; the other, a gaunt and lonely hill resembling a skull, is outside the ancient walls.

I made my way to the top of the latter site, and from this barren knoll I looked toward Jerusalem. Whether this particular spot that guides point out today is where he was crucified is beside the point. From here the vision of Christianity is clear. It is the religion of the revelation of God in Jesus Christ, and were it not for him, it would be just another faith.

Unfolding Christianity

From Golgotha the Christian story unfolds as on a screen. You see the lowly Galilean as Son of God and Son of man. You recognize him as the historical Jesus, working at his father's trade until the momentous day when he heard John the Baptist calling people to repent and proclaiming the coming of the Kingdom. When he comes to John to be baptized, Jesus has this wonderful assurance from the Father: "This is my beloved Son . . ." (Matthew 3:17). You see him as the living Christ, a divine reality working in the world today. Brought into the world and pervading it by the grace of God, he is sustained in the world by his mystical Body, which is the Church of true believers.

From Golgotha you see him through the teachings of your

faith and through your vision, wisdom, hope, and inner longing, and that is why he is seen differently by different individuals. He came to fulfill the Law. For some he was a
Jew who never traveled very far from the Jewish faith. To
others he was a revolutionist against Judaism. To still others
he was the Exemplary Man. To those who really knew him
in the New Testament sense he was God incarnate.

You see it all from Golgotha. You see Christianity with
its variegated followers—850,000,000, largest among all the
religions of the world. You see its 250,000 churches in the
United States and its more than 250 denominational expressions. You see its schools, hospitals, homes, its great cathe-
drals, its lowly missions, its city chapels, and its wayside
shrines. You see it in Rome and Moscow, in peace and war,
in joy and in sorrow. Wherever and whenever man's highest
relationship with God is contemplated, there Christianity is
found. Christianity is the religion of the revelation of God
in Christ.

More Than a Prophet

Christ was different and distinctive among prophets and
religious teachers. He spoke with authority unlike that of
any man. The Fatherhood of God showed forth in him. The
brotherhood of man was revealed in him. He taught the meaning of sin, repentance, and forgiveness. He demonstrated
neighborliness and nonresistance. He revealed the deepest
insights into rewards and punishments. He brought a noble,
persuasive gospel, using a child as an illustration of faith,
a shepherd as a symbol of love, and a lowly Samaritan as an
example of selfless service.

He had prophecies for those who benefited from them,
signs for those who wanted them, and miracles for those who

needed them. But for those who caught the glory of his presence, there was always the challenge to higher living and greater trust in God.

Look down into Jerusalem from Golgotha, and you can imagine what our Savior's triumphal march into the Temple area on that first Palm Sunday was like. You will remember the Feast of the Passover, the plot against him, the betrayal, arrest, trial, the release of Barabbas, and the Crucifixion by the Romans on a hill where criminals were ignominiously put to death. Perhaps it was here, here on this Golgotha, that his cross was lifted up. It was here, probably, that he looked out upon the world and up into the heart of God; it was here that he spoke the seven last words.

Throughout the hundreds of years that have passed since darkness fell over the city at the death of God's Anointed One, interpreters have been trying to define exactly what Christianity is, what it implies, and how it stands in relationship to other religions of mankind. Theologians have labeled it a revealed religion, a religion of regeneration and redemption, an experiential religion, a religion of the Logos, a faith of doctrine and deed.

From strictest orthodoxy to liberal humanism, from the coming of the Kingdom by an instantaneous miracle to its evolvement through struggle and growth, from evangelistic stress upon self-denial to the modern emphasis upon self-realization, Christianity has many expressions. But in every case, in every school of thought, in every sectarian camp, Christianity is the religion of the revelation of God in Christ. And it does not speak of a Christ whose life and teachings were snuffed out on a hangman's hill. For the most part, this faith was founded not on the happenings of Golgotha but on what took place in a garden only a few hours later.

There the sorrowing women who had come to anoint the dead body of their beloved Master found instead an empty tomb.

THE BIRTH OF THE CHURCH

We must leave Golgotha and go to the garden. Some call it the garden tomb, others the Garden of Joseph of Arimathea. It is a quiet, sequestered spot with flowers, a well, and an empty sepulchre. It qualifies well for Christendom's remembrance of the first hallowed Easter morn. "He is not here," the Scripture says, "for he has risen, as he said." (Matthew 28:6.)

Here from the garden of the Resurrection you can look out across the Christian Era, and you can see the full sweep of Christianity in a new perspective. You realize that with all its divisions, factions, and diversities it is actually more united than we realize. It is united in the risen Christ, and, because of this, the likenesses of these groups outweigh their differences. The miracle of the garden is that all denominations and all expressions of Christianity can be assembled here, and still there is room.

There is room for the disciples from Thomas, the doubter, to impetuous Peter. Paul, the first great missionary, is here, and all the saints and martyrs of the early church are present. The followers of Christ—called "Christians" first at Antioch and recognized by their love for one another—they are here. Those who preserved the early letters of the Church—the Church Fathers—they are here also.

Walking in the garden, I felt that the so-called heretics— those who opposed the fixed dogmas of the institutionalized church—were also here. For history does not deny the fact that Christianity frequently became involved in a struggle for power—political power, state power, and world power.

All such problems were far from the intention of Jesus Christ and were greatly opposed to the simple teachings that he had proclaimed. Always there have been those who saw Christianity as God's sword to conquer the "heathen." Constantine the Great claimed that on his way to Rome at the head of his warring troops he saw, as in a vision, a flaming cross against the sky. And over the cross he saw the words, "In this sign conquer!"

Christianity became the state religion of the Roman Empire, and the Church grew. Indeed, there were centuries in which it was known as the Holy Catholic Church, and emperors were crowned and dethroned, "holy wars" were encouraged, and crusades were instigated. The idea was to "save" Christianity from pagan threats, to convert the "heathen," to capture Jerusalem, and even to find the cup from which the Christ drank at his Passover Feast with his disciples.

Schisms and Reforms

And I remembered how the vaunted Holy Catholic Church was torn by schisms and hatreds and struggles for power. In the East the mighty Byzantine Empire claimed Jesus to be the founder of its faith no less than did the Catholic Church of Rome. The latter insisted that it had primacy to the claim of the one true Church and that its pope was God's chosen vicar of Christ. The patriarch of eastern Catholicism disagreed and in 1054 excommunicated the pope of Rome, who had already sought to excommunicate the patriarch!

So what was called the one true Church became two churches, and all through the ensuing years there were followers of Christ outside the formidable walls of both these lavish kingdoms of the lowly Nazarene. Groups like the

Moravian Brethren, the Waldenses, and the Anabaptists said they, too, belonged to the true Church. Individuals of deep commitment like John Huss, John Wycliffe, Girolamo Savonarola, and Gerhard Groote were convinced that God had given them revelations, too. And there was room for all of them in the garden of the resurrected Christ.

The reformers were in the garden, too—men who wrote one of the most thrilling chapters in the march of the Christian faith. Martin Luther, the Augustinian monk, was here, challenging Roman Catholicism to define and justify its doctrines and examine its conduct in the light of scriptural truth. John Calvin, John Knox, Huldreich Zwingli, and other reformers were all here within the growing ranks of Protestantism. Protestantism—which had nothing to protest and everything to proclaim—became the passionate expression of a people's faith and, it was believed, the reinstatement of the teachings of the Christ.

Here in the garden I could understand how Protestantism, born in schism, continued to be schismatic. Created by the impulse of reform, it has followed reform tactics down through the years. It was determined to rediscover the Christ and recapture his spirit, and the rediscovery was to be continual.

One man served as an excellent example of the best and most impressive post-Reformation advocates for a purer, holier, and more consecrated life. John Wesley, dominating eighteenth-century Protestantism both in personal dedication and in the evangelistic revival, urged and inspired people to believe in the changeless gospel of Christ. He was a graduate of Oxford, a fellow of Lincoln College, a linguist, minister, and missionary; but he was first of all a dedicated man of deep commitment.

With his brother Charles, poet and writer of six thousand gospel hymns, John Wesley put into practice the principles inherent in Christ's teaching and life. By a rigid devotion to what they thought of as spiritual habits they generated a power and so inspired others to follow their example that the world nicknamed them "Methodists" because of their methodical devotion. From such a beginning and by means of the contagion of the triumphant Christian spirit the Methodist denomination came into existence. The fellowship of The Methodist Church today in America alone includes over nine million persons.

In the garden of the Resurrection we can visualize the cavalcade of the various representatives of the Christian faiths passing in review at the open tomb: members of the Eastern Orthodox Church, Roman Catholics, Copts, silent Quakers, shouting Pentecostals, and Unitarians. Who can count the members of the Christian world or estimate their potential? Whoever and wherever they are, whatever they believe and teach and seek to live, they are all part of the heritage of faith which claims a risen Lord.

The Christian Hope

No other religion presents the claim or proves the claim that Christianity has made to the world. No other scripture leads men away from the garden tomb as confidently and as beautifully as does the Christian story: "Then he led them out as far as Bethany, and lifting up his hands he blessed them. While he blessed them, he parted from them." (Luke 24:50-51.) "And while they were gazing into heaven as he went, behold, two men stood by them in white robes, and said, 'Men of Galilee, why do you stand looking into heaven? This Jesus, who was taken up from you into heaven, will come in the same way as you saw him go into heaven." (Acts 1:10-11.)

This, too, is the Christian hope—that Jesus Christ will come again. And this, also, is interpreted in countless ways by the 850,000,000 citizens of Christendom. Their views are many; their opinions are varied and strongly individualized. But in the deepest spirit of their quest there is a basic, irrevocable agreement. A united conviction is expressed in a universally accepted and dearly loved text that every Christian knows, respects, and believes, "For God so loved the world that he gave his only Son, that whoever believes in him should not perish but have eternal life." (John 3:16.)

Christianity is the religion of the revelation of God in Christ.

10

Your Religion and You

WHENEVER I return from a journey into another religious culture and again see our beautiful churches here in America, and when I remember our freedom of worship and recognize the spiritual heritage of our Christian faith, there comes to mind a famous religious classic. It is called *Acres of Diamonds* and was written around seventy years ago by Russell Conwell. It tells the story of a man who searched the world for riches, never realizing that treasures were buried in his own back yard.

OUR GREATEST POSSESSION

Spiritually speaking, Conwell's story is a parable that applies to many of us. Intrigued by tantalizing reports of foreign faiths, lured by hope of some easy, miraculous discovery, or enticed by the promise of some mystical fulfillment, some of us may have felt that we needed to seek further for pearls of great price.

This book has been an excursion that has taken us among many persons of other faiths. It has alerted us to the world's heritage of faith and has provided us with clues to the merits and virtues of beliefs people live by. The story of man's

121

quest is life's most fascinating story, and many times, as we walked the path with a true believer, we have said, "This is a technique I can use. This is a concept I can employ. Here is a new revelation." But when the journey is complete, we return from our search to discover even greater treasures hidden in our own faith.

As I say this, I realize that there is indeed a great deal that the world's religions can teach us. There is immense good in all of them, as we have seen. The major emphasis in each is worthy of the solemn consideration of every man. God has spread his truth liberally and with a generous hand. "He made from one every nation of men to live on all the face of the earth . . . ." (Acts 17-26.)

When we visit other lands and learn about other religions, we discover that every faith has something distinctive and something of which to be proud. But our greatest treasure is hidden in our own faith.

The trouble is that too few of us dig deeply enough, work hard enough, or believe with sufficient devotion that our religion is God's special revelation for us. I believe strongly in research among people of other religions. I think that persons are wise when they visit people of other lands. I advocate strongly a sympathetic understanding of the other person's point of view. But, most important of all, I feel that we should mine first the acres of diamonds in our own expression of the Christian faith.

Working at Our Faith

We often lose the deepest perspective of our heritage because we are so near to it. We let our faith become commonplace, and we therefore settle for mediocrity. We lose the spirit of adventure. What we have obtained too easily, we hold too lightly. We forget, perhaps, this great inescapable truth: What religion is and does for us depends upon us. Faith works only when we put it into action.

Many times in my research, when I am boldly interviewing the follower of some ancient creed and ask him a particularly difficult question about his belief, I instinctively ask myself, "What if he were to ask me about *my* religion? What would I say? What would he see in me as far as my relationship with God is concerned?"

Let us look at our thinking for a moment. What if a Hindu or a Buddhist came to us and said, "Tell me what Methodism is and does. What is its philosophy? What do you live by?" Or what would happen if a Parsi, a Jew, or a Confucianist stood before us and asked, "What does your religion have to say about evil and suffering in the world? What are its claims to greatness among the world's great religions?"

A Shintoist might ask us, "What is the basis of joy in your faith?" And a Moslem might well wish to know about our church's connection with historic Christianity. He might wonder what we truly believe about Christ, about the meaning of the sacraments, and about the significance of our ritual.

Not only are professed followers of religious movements asking questions, but others are asking them, too. Of the nearly three billion people in the world, approximately 500,-000,000 have no affiliation with institutionalized religion. Many of them want to know whether the professedly religious person really finds life more rewarding than does the man who makes no religious claims. They wonder about what a person's faith does for him in times of trouble, in seasons of joy or concern, and in times of abundance. They may ask in what ways our lives are richer, more secure, or more productive because of our religious beliefs.

If we are wise and honest, we will study not only the faiths of others, but we will resolve to invest a greater part of ourselves and our thinking in our own faith.

CHRISTIANITY—THE FINAL REVELATION OF GOD

Let us take a new look at our heritage. Let us ask ourselves, "What have *I* found? When am *I* going to explore the deepest reaches of *my* religion?"

My research has proved that no other religion has as complete a revelation of God as has Christianity. No other faith offers men what we find in Jesus Christ—the Way, the Truth, and the Life.

Whenever we undertake the slightest spiritual adventure, static religion is converted into spiritual realization. Whenever we begin to live our faith, our trust increases. Every great religious teacher presented the basic view that personal awareness of godlikeness is the beginning of spiritual wisdom, and no one phrased it more perfectly or demonstrated it more clearly than did Jesus when he said, "The kingdom of God is within you" (Luke 17:21, King James Version).

It is a mistake to think that Jesus is not divine because he taught truths that had been presented by prophets and holy men before his coming. We must not be offended if someone says that the golden rule is not original in Christianity or that beatitudes and commandments have been presented by other religions before the time of Christ. Truth is universal and timeless. Though Jesus reiterated old truths, he gave them new substance by actually living them out in his own life. In a sense he proved truth by demonstrating it. No other world teacher has done this as he did. Jesus told men that God would provide the power *for applying truth* in their lives. This is why the Christ is so universal and why his influence continues to touch and change the great religions of the world.

Every religion we have discussed in our study has been enriched, enlightened, and ennobled because of Jesus Christ. All religious thought has taken on a deeper compassion when touched by his compassion. Persons of other faiths have become more godlike because of his godlikeness and more selfless because of his selflessness.

A PERSONAL DISCOVERY

The really significant question, however, is not, What influence has Jesus had on other faiths? Instead, it is, What has Jesus meant in *my* life?

Everyone must find God for himself, just as everyone must find his own expression of love and his own supreme joy in life. It is presumptuous and unrealistic to think we can live off the faith of another person or that we can indulge vicariously in the spiritual experience of someone else. Our admiration and applause for what others have done in the field of faith is too often merely an escape from our own commitments. It is not what others have done but what we are doing which is important. There are guides who can help us, trails that can lead us, and signposts that can direct us. There are phrases that have changed lives and ideas and secrets by which people have entered into a deeper meaning of the quest; but the actual discovery of God which will remake our world is the faith we have found for ourselves, by ourselves, and through ourselves in a deeper, more realistic fellowship with the Christ.

Regardless of where the faith is practiced, if it is really practiced in spirit and in truth, Jesus Christ is there. The challenge always comes back to the individual worshiper—

to us. Always there is the reminder that the great principles of religion do not live from generation to generation just because they are right or true or even because they were inspired by great leaders. They must be built into the structure of every new generation through individual lives.

Let us respect, admire, and appreciate the living religions of the world. Let us also enter sympathetically into the universal quest. But let us never forget that it is only when our own faith has become a vital, living, personal experience, only when we are rooted and grounded in the full inspiration and teaching of our church, only when our religion becomes our joy, that we will find the treasure, the pearl of great price, which is in our own back yard. When this happens, our world will be remade, and we can begin, if we wish, to help remake the world.

Acres of Diamonds, 121
Ahura-Mazda, 32, 37-41
Akabya ben Mahalalel (quotation), 65-66
Allah, 95, 98, 103, 107
Amesha-Spenta(s), 32, 37-41
Analects, 81-83
Ancestor worship, 81
Atman, the soul or only true self, 23; as described in the Upanishads, 30
Avesta, 32, 34; quotations from, 39, 41-42; teachings of, 39, 41-42

Bhagavad-Gita, 19, 28
Bhave, Vinoba (quotation), 30
Bodhisattva, 46, 48, 50, 52, 55
Brahma, 19, 26-27
Buddha (Siddhartha Gautama), 46-58; birth and early life, 48-49; teachings on suffering, 52-53
Buddhism, 46-58; sects of, 54-55; threat to Shinto, 91

Calvin, John, 109, 118
Christ· *see* Jesus Christ
Christian Church, birth and history of, 116-119
Christianity, 109-20; compared with Confucianism, 79, 82, 83; final revelation of God, 124-25; relationship to Judaism, 69-70; relationship to Zoroastrianism, 33-35, 36, 42
Confucianism, 73-83; Five Constant Virtues, 82-83
Confucius, 73-83; quotations, 76, 78, 79, 80, 81, 82
Conwell, Russell, 121
Crescas, Hasdai, his fourteen points for Judaism's spiritual course, 70-71

Death· Buddhist concept of, 51; Confucius' answer concerning, 76; Shinto view of, 93; Zoroastrian idea of, 42, 44-45
Diaspora, 59, 67

Eckhart, Meister, 23
Einstein, Albert, 17
Emperor worship, 88-90
Evil: Buddhist view of, 52; Zoroastrian concept of, 38-41

Fire, significance in Zoroastrianism, 42-44
Five Constant Virtues of Confucianism, 82-83
Five Pillars of Faith for Moslems, 106-7

Gandhi, Mohandas K., 30
God: Buddhist view of, 55; Christian names for, 26; Hindu belief concern-ing, 25-27; Hindu prayer to, 31; in other religions, 15; Jewish beliefs concerning, 64-65, 70-71; relationship of Jews to, 62-65, 67-71; Shinto view of, 88; universal search for, 11-12, 16; Zoroastrian teachings concerning, 37-41; *see also* Yahweh
Gods, Hindu, 26; Shinto, 86-88

Heaven, Buddha's teaching on, 57-58
Hillel, Rabbi (quotation), 65
Hinduism: 19-31; great interpreters of, 31; holy writings of, 27-30
Holy days, in Judaism, 67-69
Holy Heptad, 32, 37
Huss, John, 109, 118

Identification, Hindu law of, 22-23
Immortality, in Zoroastrianism, 38, 42; in Judaism, 71
India, 21, 22
Islam, 95-108

Jesus Christ: as ever-present Lord, 13-14; Koran references to, 104; life and teachings of, 111-120; as supreme revelation of God, 13; relationship of teachings to Zoroastrianism, 34, 36
Judaism. 59-72; ceremonial observances and holy days, 62, 67-69; definition of, 59; heritage of, 63-64; idea of suffering in, 66-67; relationship to Zoroastrianism, 33-34; types of, 71-72

Kami, 86-88
Karma: definition of, 19, 23-25; an explanation for all life's experiences, 24; in the Upanishads, 30
Knox, John, 109, 118
Koran, 95, 98-99, 102-8; quotations from, 98, 102-3, 108
Krishna, 19, 21, 26, 28

Lao-tzu, 73, 80-82

Maimonides (Rabbi Moses ben Maimon), basic concepts of, 70
Man, Buddhist idea of, 50
Marco Polo (quotation), 89
Methodism, 119
Mohammed, 96, 99, 101-3; *see also* Ubu'l Kassim
Moslem sects, 105-6

Nehru, Jawaharlal, 31
Nirvana, 46, 55

Parsi(s), 32, 35, 37
Passover, 59, 67
Pentateuch, 59, 62-63
Pentecost, 59, 68
Pitaka(s), 46, 56-58

Prayer, Moslem emphasis on, 98
Purim, 59, 68

Ramayana, 28
Reformers, Christian, 118
Reincarnation: Hindu definition of, 25;
  in the Upanishads, 30
Religion: its different meanings, 14-15;
  new demands upon, 16; a universal
  search, 18
Resurrection: basic to Christian faith,
  115-16; Jewish belief in, 70
Rig-Veda, 29
Rishis, 28
Rosh Hashana, 59, 67-68

Sacred Seven (Zoroastrianism), 37-38
Sacred writings: of Buddhism (quo-
  tations), 50-51, 56-58; of Christianity
  (quotations), 111-13, 119, 122, 124;
  of Confucianism, 81-83; of Hinduism,
  27-30; of Judaism, 62-63, 64-66; of
  Taoism, 81-83; of Zoroastrianism, 34,
  41-42
Sarnath murals, 47-49, 52
Schweitzer, Albert, 17-18
Seder, 59, 67
Shinto, 84-94
Siddhartha Gautama, 48-50; see also
  Buddha
Six Articles of Belief in Islam, 107

Soul, as defined by a Hindu, 23
Seven Satans, 40
Suffering, Buddha's ideas concerning
  49, 51-53; of the Jews, 66-67

Tagore, Rabindranath, 31
Talmud, 60, 65-66
Tao Te Ching, 81-82
Taoism, 73, 80-83
Torah, 60, 64-65
Toynbee, Arnold, 15

Ubu'l Kassim, 99-101; see also Mo
  hammed
Upanishads, 20, 29-30

Veda(s), 20, 28-29
Vedanta, another name for Upanishads
  29

Wesley, Charles, 118
Wesley, John, 118
Worship, a universal desire, 16
Wycliffe, John, 110, 118

Yahweh, 60, 64-65

Zoroaster, Spitama, 32; death of, 43
  early life of, 35-37; parents of, 35
  teachings of, 33-35, 37-41; see also
  Zoroastrianism
Zoroastrianism, 32-45

CPSIA information can be obtained
at www.ICGtesting.com
Printed in the USA
BVHW052022080521
606756BV00003B/380

9 780343 232061